WOODWORKING
TECHNIQUES

WOODWORKING
TECHNIQUES

**Best methods
for building
furniture from
*Fine Woodworking***

The Taunton Press

essentials of woodworking

Special thanks to the editors, art directors, copy editors,
and other staff members of *Fine Woodworking* who contributed to
the development of the articles in this book.

Front cover photo by Charley Robinson
Back cover photos by William Duckworth (top left),
Vincent Laurence (top right), Gary Straub (bottom)

The Taunton Press
Inspiration for hands-on living™

© 2000 by The Taunton Press, Inc.
All rights reserved.

Printed in the United States of America
10 9 8 7 6 5 4

The Taunton Press, Inc., 63 South Main Street, PO Box 5506,
Newtown, CT 06470-5506
e-mail: tp@taunton.com

Distributed by Publishers Group West

Library of Congress Cataloging-in-Publication Data

Woodworking techniques / best methods for building furniture from Fine woodworking.
    p. cm.—(Essentials of woodworking)
  Includes index.
  ISBN 1-56158-345-6
  1. Furniture making—Amateurs' manuals. I. Series.

TT195.W67 2000
684'.08—dc21   99-047527

About Your Safety
Working with wood is inherently dangerous. Using hand or power tools improperly or ignoring
standard safety practices can lead to permanent injury or even death. Don't try to perform operations you
learn about here (or elsewhere) unless you're certain they are safe for you. If something about an
operation doesn't feel right, don't do it. Look for another way. We want you to enjoy the craft,
so please keep safety foremost in your mind whenever you're working with wood.

"The lyfe so short, the craft so long to lerne, Th' assay so hard, so sharpe the conquering."

—GEOFFREY CHAUCER

CONTENTS

INTRODUCTION

Great woodworking skills cannot be bought. Only a lifetime of application will give a woodworker the ability to do a complex job quickly, efficiently, and perfectly with few second thoughts and the greatest of ease. Though these skills are amazing to watch, they are much more enjoyable when experienced first hand.

Woodworking Techniques shows the work of some of these masters. They offer the fruits of their experience, which are the very best methods and approaches to making furniture. These are the "little skills" that woodworkers use every day in their shops—how to set a hinge, how to taper a leg, and how to fit a drawer.

To the inexperienced, this work can be tremendously time-consuming and frustrating. One lock might require several test pieces, lots of fussing and fiddling, and many mistakes to repair along the way. Then it may never come out perfectly centered. But instead of reinventing the wheel and teaching yourself through trial and error, follow Phil Lowe's instructions and learn a great way to do it. Results are never guaranteed the first time, but after some practice, they are.

Teaching these skills is a skill in itself, of course. It's often said that those who can't do something teach it instead. This may contain a grain of truth for professions where demonstration isn't essential to teaching, but it isn't the case in woodworking. The only way to teach woodworking is to show it being done. All aspects of the work become evident: what comes first, how to hold your hands, how much pressure to apply, etc.

The best woodworking teachers know how to describe what they're doing, so the student's attention is brought to the most important parts. This is the central challenge of any magazine or book. Unlike a live demonstration, a book can only offer snapshots of the action and a number of words about them. But you'll find more than enough in this book to learn a new and valuable skill. The techniques presented in this book have experts behind them all conspiring to help other woodworkers get it, and get it right.

ONE

Tables

If there's more than one way to skin a cat, then there are at least three ways to taper a leg. On second thought, there are probably many more, with variations on each. For example, you may cut a taper on the bandsaw, but you still can choose between a sharp handplane, a router, or any number of sanding tools to clean up the face. The possibilities grow almost endlessly.

To beginners, this multiplicity of techniques quickly annoys. "Stop!" they call out to the experts. "Just tell me which way is best!" Sometimes they get answers, but anything definitive is always partial. Though there are better and worse methods, there is rarely a best. It often comes down to what your first teacher tells you to do, and what you learn to do well. In other words, it comes down to skill. A woodworker with tremendous bandsaw and handplane skills should use those tools to taper legs. A woodworker who knows his table saw well and can make jigs like lightning is better served with those tools. Neither route is intrinsically better. But there is a best route for you, and it depends largely on your unique set of skills.

Patrick Nelson's technique is a variation on Stickley's for making legs with quartersawn grain on all four sides. Is Nelson's technique better? In this case it is. Nelson found a way to do the work with one shaper setup instead of two. Only strident reproductionists would find fault with the technique because it isn't original. Here is a rare case of better.

The balance of sections offers ways to cut sliding dovetail slots in round table pedestals, to join legs to a tabletop with wedged-through mortise and tenons hidden by butterfly keys, and to make a round table apron with laminated bending plywood. Each technique is the result of many years of testing, fiddling, and improving. If you've never tried to make these things, these are excellent techniques to get you started. But if you have, let yourself be surprised to see it done a new way; read it through and give it a chance. Old dogs really can learn new ways to skin cats, so to speak.

THREE RELIABLE WAYS TO TAPER A LEG

by Gary Rogowski

Bandsawn tapers are safe and simple. Feed the leg blank slowly with one hand, steering as you go, and use the other hand to help guide the cut. Cut to the waste side of the line.

Table or desk legs that have been tapered top to bottom have a grace and delicacy that square legs just don't seem to have. Shaker furnituremakers exploited this leg style, and so have many others. Although legs may be tapered all the way around, more often than not I cut tapers on two adjoining faces of a leg. The process can be both quick and reliable.

Roughing out tapers is best done by machine; either a bandsaw or a tablesaw is a good choice. Tapers also can be cut by mounting leg blanks on a jig that's passed through a thickness planer, a process that requires very little cleanup. Cleaning up the cuts also can be accomplished in a number of ways—on a jointer, with a router and a flush-trimming bit, or with a handplane.

How much taper a leg gets and which faces are tapered are personal choices best made with plenty of experimentation.

1 Tapering on the bandsaw

By far, the simplest and safest way to cut a taper is to draw lines on two adjacent faces of each leg and cut just to the waste side of the lines on a bandsaw, making straight cuts (see the photo on the facing page).

The cut is not that difficult to make if your bandsaw is properly tuned and the blade is sharp. Mark out the taper on a milled leg blank, striking a line from the widest point, where the taper starts, to its narrowest point at the foot. If there's a flat near the top of the leg where an apron will intersect it, strike a line across the face of the leg where the taper begins or just slightly below it. The idea

is to leave enough material on the leg so it can be cleaned up without making the leg too thin.

If the leg shape is one you might reproduce often, consider making a template of ¼-in.-thick hardboard or medium-density fiberboard. The next time you need to lay out this taper, it will take just a few seconds.

It's easier to sight down the layout line if you lower your head a bit as you make the cut. Use two hands to help guide the leg through the blade, feed slowly and try to compensate for any drift before you wander from the line. With practice, it becomes quite easy to cut a straight line on the bandsaw. But be careful to keep your fingers out of the way. It's easy to run your thumb into a bandsaw blade.

All four legs of a table can be tapered at once. The author's planer jig is made from a piece of ¾-in.-thick plywood and three angled strips of wood to support the legs. Stops at either end of the plywood keep the legs in place.

A tapered sled jig for the planer

Front and back stops prevent the leg blank from moving in the jig. Angled support pieces keep the blanks from flexing.

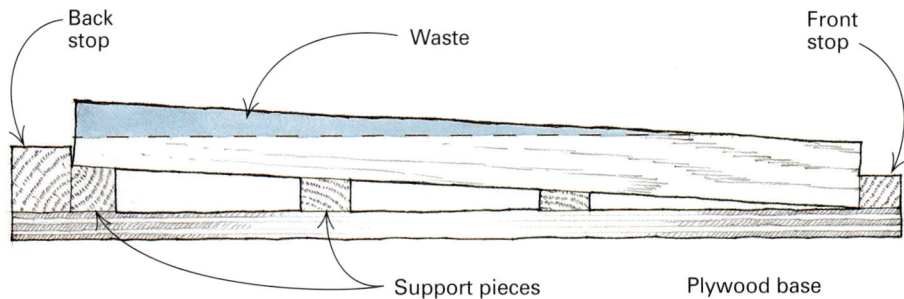

Back stop

Waste

Front stop

Support pieces

Plywood base

2 Tapering with a thickness planer

A thickness planer isn't the first tool that comes to mind for cutting tapers. But a planer will do an absolutely consistent job of tapering leg stock if you use the proper jig—one with a simple carriage that supports the legs at an angle and has stops at either end (see the photo on p. 7). The only real drawback is that it's fairly slow.

I made my jig from a piece of scrap plywood several inches longer than the length of the legs. To get the taper I wanted, I drew the taper on one of the legs, placed the leg on the plywood base of the jig and raised one end until the taper line was parallel with the plywood. I measured this height near one end of the plywood, cut a support piece to fit there and glued it on. I added a stop just behind it. The narrow end of the legs butt against this stop.

The next step is to cut angled pieces that will support the legs and prevent them from flexing under the pressure of the feed rollers in the planer. With these supports glued to the plywood base, I added another stop at the front end of the jig to capture the legs securely—I didn't want the stock moving around beneath the cutterhead.

The best thing about this method of tapering legs is that all the legs for a project can be done at the same time. Take light passes, especially at first, to minimize deflection of the stock. Also, make sure the legs don't rock on the support pieces. If they do, you'll see some vicious sniping.

3 Tablesaw tapering

The most commonly used tool for cutting tapers is the tablesaw—and why not? It's fast and, if the saw is well-tuned, very little cleanup is needed. You can either make a dedicated jig every time you need a different taper, or you can use a hinged, universal tapering jig to cut many different tapers. I prefer using dedicated jigs because I often reproduce designs (see the photo on the facing page). With a dedicated jig, I'm assured of getting the same results every time.

The base of the jig is a straight, flat piece of plywood just a few inches longer than the leg stock. I cut it so its sides are parallel and its ends are square. Then I screw a back stop to one end to catch the wide part of the taper (see the drawing above). A front stop, near the other end of the jig, captures

Tablesawn tapers are fast and accurate. A dedicated jig like this one produces consistent results but is limited to a single angle and leg length.

the leg and cants it from the plywood at the correct angle for the desired taper.

To set up for the cut, measure from the inside edge of the jig to the widest part of the taper—either the corner of the leg if it's a full-length taper or a few inches shy of the corner if you want to leave a flat section on the leg for an apron. Use this measurement to set the distance from blade to fence. Keep the jig firmly against the fence, and feed steadily as you make the cut, running the narrow end of the leg into the blade first. For the second taper on a leg, rotate the leg blank 90° clockwise in the jig. By rotating the leg this way, a square, untapered face will rest on the tablesaw.

A dedicated tablesaw jig for tapers

The front stop is rabbeted to fit securely against the plywood jig. A second rabbet holds the leg in place. A snug fit is essential.

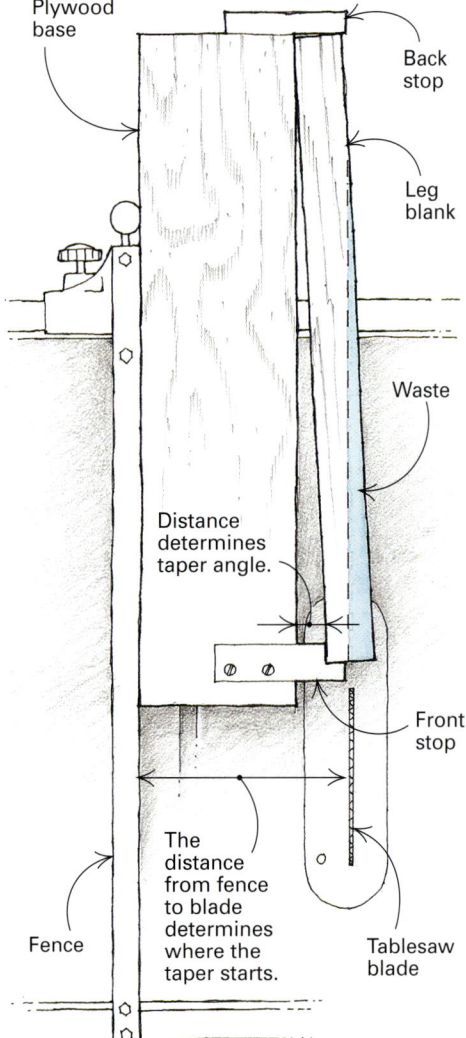

Plywood base

Back stop

Leg blank

Waste

Distance determines taper angle.

Front stop

The distance from fence to blade determines where the taper starts.

Fence

Tablesaw blade

Three ways to clean up the cuts

Some cleanup is almost always required after you've cut the basic tapers. Even a planer can leave mill marks. Here are three simple methods for cleaning tapers.

Jointer

This tool does a great job of cleaning up sawmarks (see the left photo on the facing page). I generally go straight from the bandsaw to the jointer. I set the infeed table for a light cut and use a push stick.

To avoid tearout, you should cut with the grain. That usually means the narrow end of the leg is last to go over the cutterhead. Inspect the taper first, though, checking for grain direction as well as for any high spots that may need to be taken down by hand before you joint the whole length of the taper.

Check, too, to see if one end or another needs more wood removed. You may be able to take slightly more off one end than another by varying the amount of hand pressure you apply. Make sure the tapers are well marked so you can tell when you're finished. Feed slowly to minimize cutterhead marks.

Router

A flush-trimming bit mounted in a router table is another quick way of cleaning up tapers, especially if you don't have a jointer (see the top right photo on the facing page). This technique also guarantees that all the tapers are precisely the same. Both top-bearing and bottom-bearing bits will do the job, and you can use the same templates here that you used to lay out tapers for the bandsaw. Double-faced tape works well to attach the template to each leg. For a production run, a jig with attached toggle clamps is better and faster.

When a bottom-bearing bit is used in a router table, you will have to make a tapered template for the second taper so the router bearing (which is at a fixed

Jointer cleans up tapers quickly. A few light passes over the jointer should clean up any mill marks or other surface irregularities left after roughing out a leg by machine.

Template routing ensures consistent results. Both bottom-bearing bits (shown above) and top-bearing bits work. Double-faced tape secures the template to the legs.

height) has something to ride on. You'll need thicker stock for this template.

Cut and clean up the first taper. Then mark the second taper on the template stock by placing it on the tapered leg and setting them both on a flat surface, like a bench or jointer bed. On the template stock, mark a line that's parallel with the bench or bed. Then cut and clean this second side. The template is ready for use.

Make sure the tapers have been cut close to the template shape; there shouldn't be more than $\frac{1}{16}$ in. of wood to clean up with the router. Set the height of the bit so that the bearing rides firmly against the template. Start the cut back just a little from the end of the leg. Work from the widest part of the taper to the narrowest. Rout the full length, and finish up with one smoothing pass.

Handplane

On wood that's not particularly gnarly, a well-tuned handplane can be used to clean up tapers straight off the bandsaw, planer or tablesaw. A plane also is a good choice for tapers that have been cleaned up with a jointer or router but still need a little more polishing.

Handplane cleans tapers efficiently. A plane leaves a surface that's ready for finish, but take care to plane with the grain to avoid tearout.

You'll want to plane downhill (from the wide part of the taper to the narrow), but you should check the grain direction of each face you're planing to be sure. The grain may surprise you. Make sure your stop or bench dog won't interfere with the plane at the end of its stroke. Mark a line across your stock at the start of the taper, and take lighter passes as you approach it (see the bottom photo above).

STICKLEY-STYLE LEGS

by Patrick Nelson

Quartersawn oak is synonymous with Craftsman furniture. The wood's wild ray figure is both beautiful and distinctive. Unfortunately, Mother Nature saw fit to put it only on opposing faces of a board. So on a table leg, for example, the sides adjacent to a quartersawn face should be flatsawn and without figure.

However, if you look closely at much of the furniture built by the Stickleys in the early 1900s, you'll see what looks like a freak of nature: quartersawn figure on all four sides of square table legs (see the photo at left). This figure is the result of a unique leg design used in Stickley factories.

The Stickleys used two techniques. One was to cover the flatsawn faces with quartersawn veneer. The other technique mated four quartersawn boards with trapezoidal profiles. The base of each trapezoid was one face of the leg, and the two adjacent sides were angled at 45°. On one angled side, there was a small perpendicular notch; on the other side was a complementary tooth. Mating tooth to notch on adjacent pieces lined up the four joints perfectly.

Freak of nature? No, just a bit of technical wizardry. Quartersawn figure occurs naturally only on opposing faces of a board, but the legs on many Craftsman pieces show it all around. The author used one router bit and two jigs to make the leg shown above.

One modern bit does the trick

The shaper bits used to mill the original Stickley design are not commonly available today, but the widely available lock-miter router bit can be used to make these Stickley-style legs. The bit is beveled at 45°, like a large chamfer bit, with a pair of opposing teeth in the middle of the cutting surface. It cuts a profile that's quite similar to the one used by the Stickleys. I bought my bit from Grizzly Imports (P.O. Box 2069, Bellingham, WA 98227; 800-541-5537). They're also sold by a number of other router-bit manufacturers.

The lock-miter bit actually has some advantages over the shaper cutters used by the Stickleys: This bit produces a joint with a larger glue-surface area, only one is needed to cut both sides of the joint, and just one setup is required. Adjusting the lock-miter bit height and the position of the fence to get that setting is just trial-and-error. You can get pretty close right from the start, though, by centering one of the teeth on the stock. And once you have the setting right, the actual routing takes just a few minutes.

I mount the bit in my shaper rather than in a router table. The shaper's slower speed is less intimidating than a router with a bit of this size. But if you don't have a shaper, the technique would work using a powerful, variable-speed router set at its slowest speed. The key to the technique is the pair of jigs I made to hold the workpieces as they're fed through the bit (see the drawings on p. 14).

One jig for each pass

The first jig holds the workpiece flat against the table and exposes the edge of the workpiece to the router. The jig is made of two pieces of plywood with pine end caps. The end caps start out as rectangular pieces but take on the lock-miter profile after the first pass. Screws driven through the end caps, far enough back to be out of the bit's way, hold the workpiece in place (see the left drawing on p. 14). The distance from the edge of the narrower piece of plywood, against which the workpiece butts, to the edge of the wider piece, which rides against the fence, is the width of the leg. It's easy to make the legs any size you want.

Quartersawn figure on all four sides _____

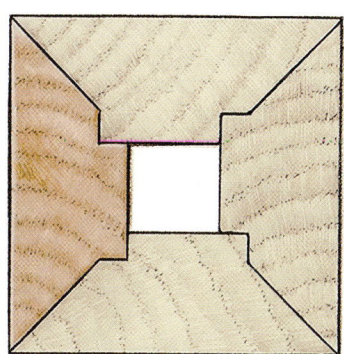

Stickley method

On original Stickley pieces, the leg was made up of four pieces. Each of these pieces had two complementary profiles cut into it using two shaper setups.

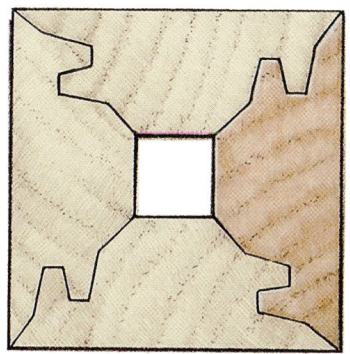

Author's version

The author's version of the Stickley leg is made up of four identical pieces. The edge profile on each piece mates with the face profile on an adjacent piece.

First jig, first pass ——————

One jig positions workpiece flat on table to cut the profile on edge of stock.

Inside edge rides against shaper or router-table fence.

Offset between two pieces of plywood is width of leg.

Pine end cap

Screws hold end cap in place. Screw in workpiece is positioned out of the way of the bit.

Second jig, second pass ——————

Second jig positions workpiece vertically to cut the profile on the inside face.

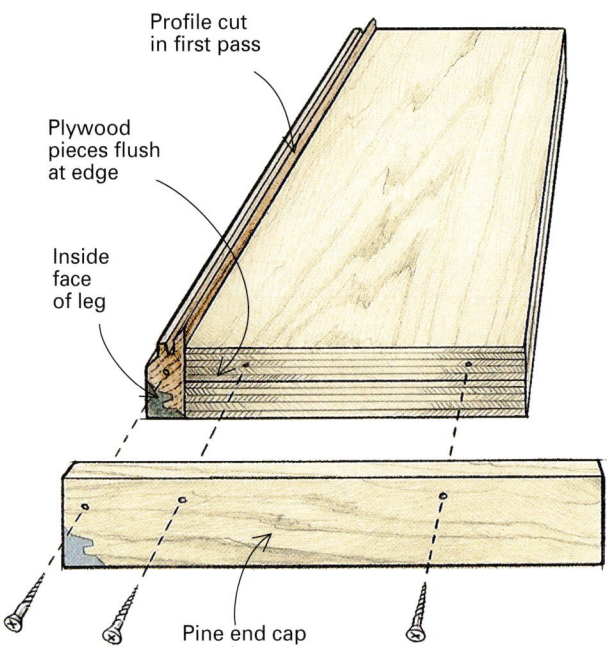

Profile cut in first pass

Plywood pieces flush at edge

Inside face of leg

Pine end cap

Stock from $\frac{9}{16}$ in. thick on up to 1 in. or $1\frac{1}{4}$ in. (depending on the make of the bit) can be used with the lock-miter bit, but the thickness of the parts of the jig and the stock you're using for the pieces that will make up the leg must be identical. I dimensioned stock to the thickness of the shop-grade plywood (nominally $\frac{3}{4}$ in.) that I used for the jig. It was easier than building up each layer of the jig from multiple pieces of plywood or milling the pieces of the jig from solid wood. I also crosscut the leg stock and jig stock at the same time, so their lengths are identical.

The second jig looks similar to the first one. But the two pieces of plywood are the same size, and they are flush on their edges (see the right drawing above). The work-

piece is held vertically against the edges of the plywood. This way, the inner face of the workpiece is presented to the router bit.

After the workpiece has passed through the router bit in this second jig, the workpiece will have identical profiles on one edge and on the inside face. Each leg is made up of four such pieces, one edge of each piece mating with the face of the adjacent piece, all the way around the leg. I always make the legs several inches longer than they will be on the finished piece of furniture so that I can trim off the ends after the leg has been assembled.

These legs can be used on many different kinds of furniture, and the process of making a leg is the same, regardless of size or what the leg will be used for.

Rout the edge profile first. Maintain a steady feed rate, and keep pressure against the fence. Each profile is cut in a single pass.

Rout the inside face of the leg stock. The piece should be edge up with its outside face against the jig (above). After the second pass, the piece has matching profiles on its edge and inside face (right).

Gluing Up

1. Apply glue to just two pieces of each leg at a time. Then, after you have the two halves assembled, apply glue to the remaining faces, and bring the two halves together.

2. Tack battens down center of each side. These battens will help concentrate the clamping pressure.

3. Tack one end of a bungee cord to the end of a batten.

4. Wrap cord tightly around the assembly. Tack the bungee cord at the other end.

5. Tap along the battens to make sure the joints are seated.

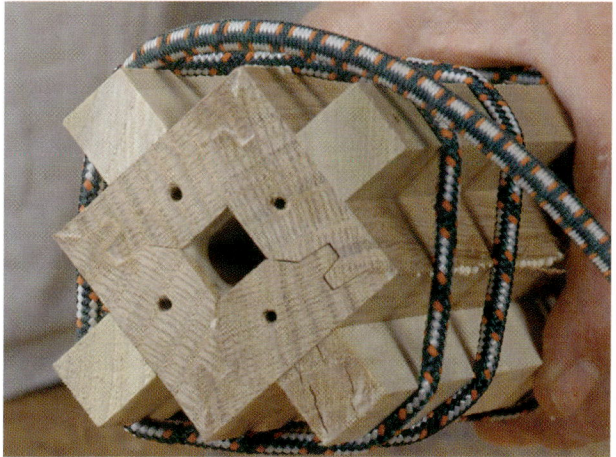

6. The wrapped assembly is set aside to let the glue cure. After a few hours, the leg can be unwrapped and the ends trimmed. This eliminates the screw holes and any slight gaps at the ends where the clamping pressure isn't as great. The leg is now ready to use.

DINING TABLE WITH TILT TOP

by Nigel Martin

Practical and versatile, this pedestal table, shown here in cherry with ebony stringing, can be made with a round or oval top, and the simple design will play as well in the den as the dining room.

The straightforward, uncluttered design of this dining table lets it fit as comfortably in a kitchen as in a formal dining room, and with its tilting top, it can be stowed against a wall in a room with multiple uses. Over the years, I've made it in cherry, as shown in the photo above, as well as chestnut, ash, elm and oak, with different finishes and detailing depending on the setting and the customer.

I think round and oval tables provide the most sociable seating arrangement, but they concentrate more knees in less space. That's why a pedestal base, with its yards of extra legroom, is such a good match for a rounded-top table. For reasons of balance and stress, a central pedestal base won't pair as well with large rectangular tops whose corners can become powerful levers. Even with a rounded top, the leg joints in a

Making a tilt-top pedestal table

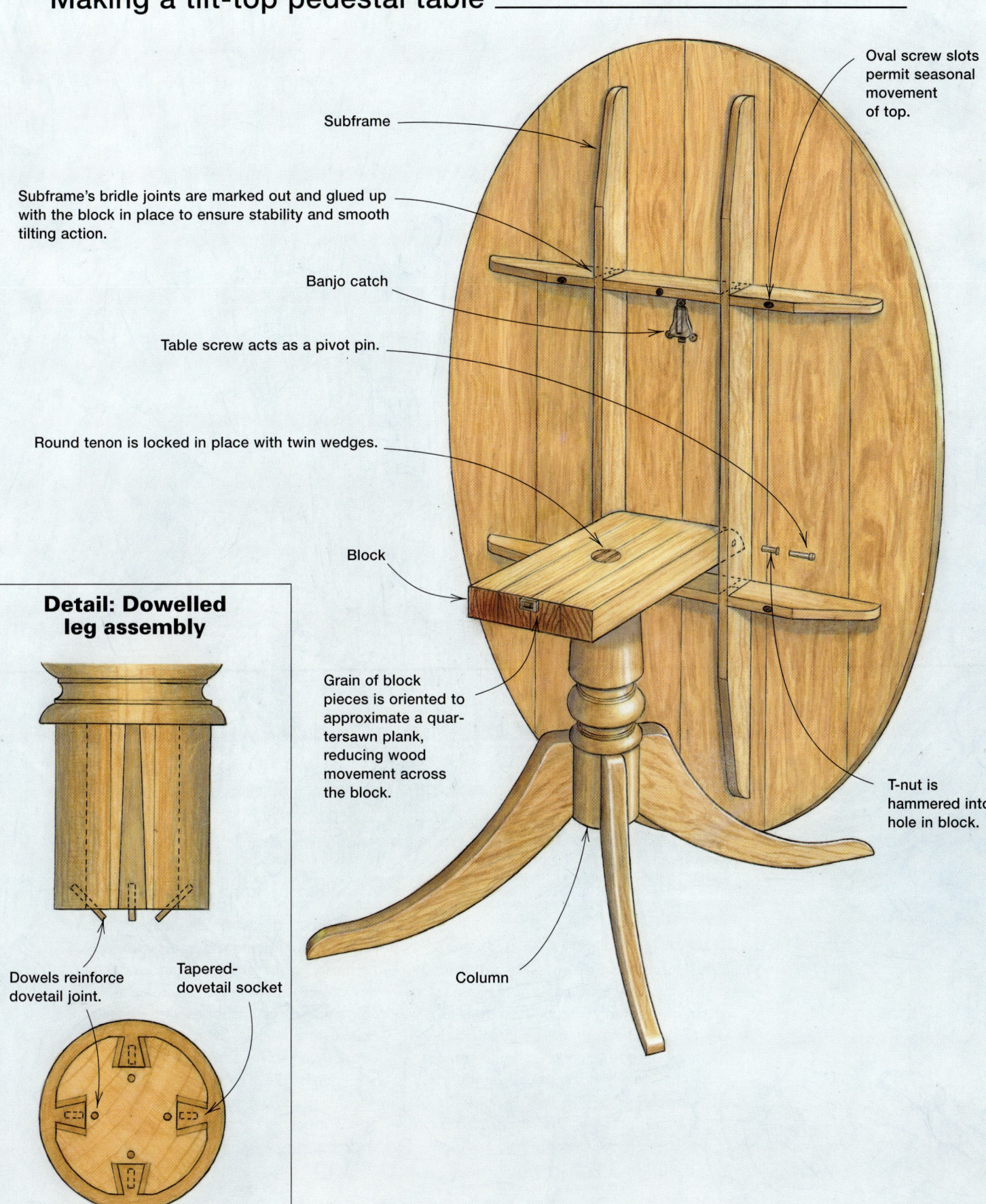

Subframe

Oval screw slots permit seasonal movement of top.

Subframe's bridle joints are marked out and glued up with the block in place to ensure stability and smooth tilting action.

Banjo catch

Table screw acts as a pivot pin.

Round tenon is locked in place with twin wedges.

Block

Grain of block pieces is oriented to approximate a quartersawn plank, reducing wood movement across the block.

T-nut is hammered into hole in block.

Column

Detail: Dowelled leg assembly

Dowels reinforce dovetail joint.

Tapered-dovetail socket

Cradle for routing flats on turned pedestal column _____

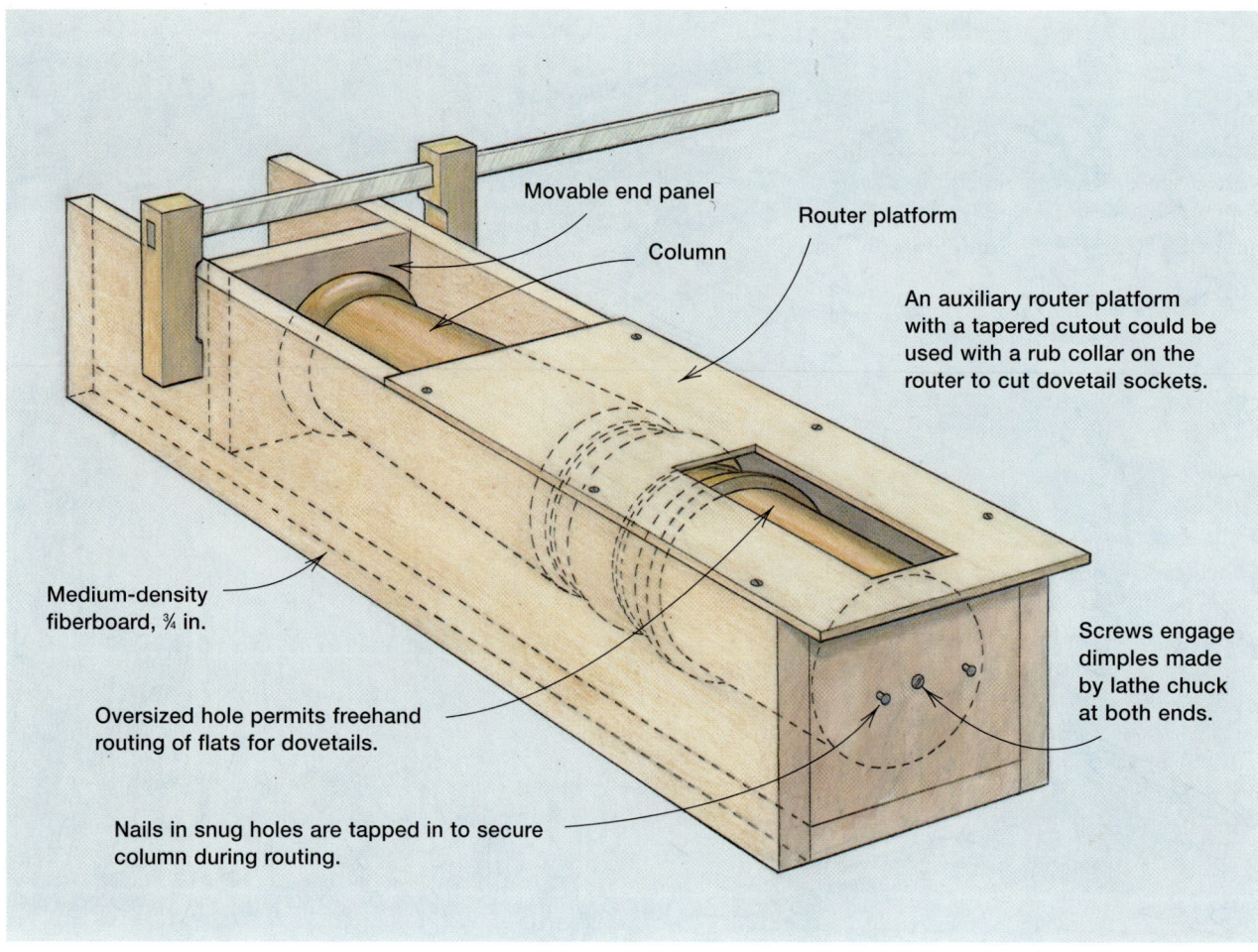

Movable end panel

Column

Router platform

An auxiliary router platform with a tapered cutout could be used with a rub collar on the router to cut dovetail sockets.

Medium-density fiberboard, ¾ in.

Oversized hole permits freehand routing of flats for dovetails.

Screws engage dimples made by lathe chuck at both ends.

Nails in snug holes are tapped in to secure column during routing.

---

pedestal are subjected to enormous stresses. To resist those stresses, I join the legs and column of this table with tapered sliding dovetails, a very strong, self-locking joint, which I reinforce with toenailed dowels, as shown in the drawing on p. 19.

Start with a drawing

I begin each table by making a full-scale, cross-section drawing on a sheet of ⅛-in. Masonite painted white to show up my lines. I draw the column, one leg, the block and a section of the top. As I build, I make notes on the Masonite and end up with all my information in one place, making for easy referral and reuse. I let the bottom edge of the Masonite be my floor line and draw

in the top of the table 29 in. above that. I work downward from there, sketching in the block and the contours of the column. When I've established the bottom line of the column, I can determine the splay of the legs. For maximum stability, the tips of the legs should extend out as far as possible. I locate the tips about 2 in. inside the rim of the tabletop. For a table with a round top, this can be accomplished on the cross-section drawing, but for an oval-topped table like this one, I draw a top view to locate the tips and then transfer the measurement of the leg span to the cross section. When I have located the tip of the foot, I draw the curve of the leg back up to the column.

Doing the legwork

Once I am happy with the shape of the leg, I make a tracing of it and then a template, adding an inch for the dovetail pin. I lay out the legs on planed stock, being careful to minimize short grain, and cut them out on the bandsaw. I clean up the bottom of the foot and the butt of the dovetail pin with a plane, making sure that they're at right angles to the sides of the leg. I fair the curves with a spokeshave and finish up with a scraper and sandpaper.

Dovetail pins

I use a simple jig clamped to the sliding table of my tablesaw to cut the tapered dovetail pins on the legs, as shown in the photo at right. A similar setup would work equally well with a miter gauge or a sliding crosscut carriage instead of a sliding table. I find that an 11° blade tilt is about right for this joint, providing excellent locking without excessive flair. To produce the appropriate taper for a 6-in. pin, I set the fence of the sliding table to 4°. I clamp the leg to the upright of the jig, making sure the butt of the dovetail is flat on the saw table. When I've cut one cheek on all four legs, I swing the fence on the sliding table to 4° the other way and then repeat the process to cut the other cheek.

Now I'm ready to make the shoulder cuts. I remove the jig, return the blade to vertical and then set the rip fence 7/8 in. from the blade (with the kerf, I'm cutting 1 in.). I lay the leg on a wedge-shaped piece of wood (whose angle corresponds to the taper of the dovetail) and clamp it to my sliding table. I push the leg through the sawblade with the butt of the pin against the rip fence, making a perfect tapered dovetail, which requires no further hand-work. The shoulder cut could also be made without the wedge beneath the leg; the saw-blade would be set lower so it only cut to the widest point of the pin's neck and then the finish cut could be quickly made with a handsaw. With the legs shaped and the pins cut, I turn to making the column.

Low-tech tenoning. A jig made from two scraps of fiberboard simplifies cutting the pins of the tapered sliding dovetails for the author's table.

Preparing the pedestal

Unless I have a suitable 6-in.-sq. billet, I laminate the pedestal column from two or three pieces of stock. I cut the billet long by about 1 in. to allow for truing cuts on the lathe at each end. After turning a cylindrical blank and squaring the ends, I mark the spinning piece with pencil lines wherever changes in the profile will occur. To transfer these transition points from the drawing, I first trace the column's profile onto a piece of white poster board. Then I strike square lines out to the edge of the cardboard from each transition point on the column. Where each one of these lateral lines meets the edge of the cardboard, I make a tiny V-notch with a pocketknife to hold the tip of a pencil.

My bead and cove designs vary, but I always turn a 2-in. round tenon at the top of the column to join the block that supports the tabletop and a 6-in. cylinder at the bottom for the leg joints.

Dovetail sockets

The first step in cutting the dovetail sockets, or housings, is creating flat areas where each leg will join the column. You could cope the shoulders of the pins to match the radius of the column, but that's more difficult and, in most cases, will actually reduce the strength of the joint. I cut the flats with a router riding on an adjustable cradle jig that holds the column, as shown in the drawing on p. 20. Once I have cut the flats, I mark out the sockets from the pins (numbering mating pins and sockets). After a cup of coffee, it's time to remove the waste from the dovetail sockets. I use my hollow chisel mortiser and the setup shown in the photo at right. You could also use a bit in a drill press or even a hand-held drill to remove most of the waste and finish up by hand.

Fitting the joints

Here's the moment of truth—the dovetail should slide right up to within $1/4$ in. to $1/2$ in. of the end of the socket. If the top of the leg is within $1/4$ in. of the end of the socket, you are probably safe to tap it gently home. When the joint is home, there should be no gaps between the shoulder and the flat on the column. If the leg is much more than $1/4$ in. from the end of the socket, remove it, and rub a soft leaded pencil on all surfaces of the pin. Then reinsert it, and remove it once more. Pencil marks will be transferred to the socket, so you can identify the high spots and pare them away with a chisel.

Once the fit of each leg is satisfactory, I smear a little yellow glue on all surfaces of the socket and tap the pin home. It is important not to overdo it with the glue: If you use too much and glue gets carried toward the shoulder, you could get a hydraulic lock that will prevent the leg from being driven home or even split the column. Once the legs are glued in, the column can be set down on the floor. No clamps are needed. When the glue dries, I reinforce the joint with dowels driven at 45° from near the center of the bottom of the column out into the butts of the dovetail pins.

Block building

I glue up the block from 2-in.- or 3-in.-wide pieces with their grain oriented so that together they approximate a quartersawn plank (as shown in the drawing on p. 19). The hole to mate with the round tenon on the top of the column can be drilled with an expansive-type bit in a drill press, or it can be turned outboard on the lathe. I round over the top edge at one end of the block to provide the clearance the tabletop needs to move through 90°. At this point, I fit the block on the pedestal without glue and set it aside. Then I turn to the table's subframe.

Subframe fit is key

For the stability of the table, it's essential that the block fit snugly between the two long rails of the subframe. To ensure a good fit, I do both the marking out and gluing up of the subframe's bridle joints with the block secured in position. I use table screws at one end of the block, where they function as pivot pins, and a single banjo catch at the other end, as shown in the drawing on p. 19. If the table is to have a fixed top, I replace the banjo catch with a second pair of table screws. Hardware for both fixed and tilt-top pedestal tables is available from Garrett Wade, 161 Avenue of the Americas, New York, N.Y., 10013; (800) 221-2942.

After gluing up the subframe, I do any necessary trimming on the edges of the block until it moves smoothly within the frame, and I glue the block to the pedestal. It's critical to orient the block accurately on the column because this will determine the relationship between top and feet. To make the match, I take the just-glued (but with no tenon wedges) pedestal and block assembly and lay it on its side on the tablesaw. When the tips of two feet as well as the whole length of one edge of the block are on the table, the two parts are in alignment. Then I drive wedges into precut slots in the pedestal's round tenon.

Top it off

The top is the final component to be made. I glue it up in one hit, placing the clamps alternately above and below the top to even out clamping forces. I use urea formaldehyde glue here instead of yellow glue, which has a tendency to creep slightly and form tiny bumps along the joint lines. A few biscuits in the edges of the boards keep them in alignment. I handplane the top flat, first using a jack plane across the grain and then a really sharp smoothing plane with the grain. I try to achieve as good a finish as possible with a smoothing plane and then go straight from that to 220-grit or 320-grit sandpaper. If the wood has been kind to me, I don't sand at all. Somehow the surface of wood seems to have more clarity and character when it has been planed than when it has been sanded.

I do all the planing and any but the finest sanding before cutting out the top. It's easier to hold the top between bench dogs with the edges and ends of the boards straight, and I also avoid tearout of the finished edge when planing cross-grain. After plotting out the oval or circle, I cut to the outside of the line with a jigsaw and refine the edge with a block plane. Marking out and fairing up the curves of the top could be done just as well with a template and router, but because I have already filled my garage with templates, I prefer to do it by hand.

With the top finished, I screw the subframe to it, allowing for movement across the top's width by slotting the holes in the frame members that span it.

The finishes you could put on this table are as varied as its uses, from French polish in the formal living room to penetrating oil in the kitchen. My favorite finish is oil because it is easy to apply, protects the wood well and, over a period of time, it develops a beautiful sheen.

Chopping the leg sockets—Three tapered shims hold the column in register as a hollow-chisel mortiser cuts the cheeks of the dovetail sockets.

JOINERY FOR LIGHT, STURDY COFFEE TABLE

by Lindsay Suter

I knew a wood supplier in California, a whacky old hippie, whose joy was salvaging trees everyone else overlooked and then turning the wood into spectacular lumber. His lumberyard may have been in complete chaos, but he had a gift for finding the raw material for truly memorable furniture. It was in these wood stacks that I found the curly cherry perfectly suited for a low coffee table I had designed.

The table shown in the photo on p. 26 looks quite simple. But its exposed joinery puts craftsmanship as well as the figured wood on display. Through tenons, wedged with butterfly keys, join the legs to the top. Narrow stretchers replace more traditional aprons, keeping the table looking light and airy. The design also is a little daring because the tabletop is fastened directly to the legs.

I wondered as I drew up the plans whether this feature might result in a split top. As it turns out, the frame of this table flexes slightly as the top expands and contracts across its width. This is a result of using relatively thin stretchers, only $\frac{1}{2}$ in. thick, that are set well below the top of the frame. Because the frame isn't absolutely rigid, the top has enough freedom of movement so it won't split. I know because the first one I made went to a client in Massachusetts where summers are hot and humid and indoor winter conditions are bone dry. The table has been there for seven years and shows no signs of a problem. Even so, I would choose a relatively stable wood for this design. Quarter-sawn white oak, nara or myrtle wood all seem like good choices to me.

Cutting mortises with a dado blade

The top is glued up from four book-matched pieces that give the table a symmetrical quality. The leg tenons penetrate the top at the two outside joint lines. The inlaid butterfly keys let into the tops of the legs not only reinforce the joints between the top boards but also wedge the leg tenons. Cutting mortises into the tabletop where the boards are joined simplifies construction.

I cut the mortises with a dado blade and a crosscut sled on the tablesaw before gluing the top pieces together (see the photo on p. 27). After testing the setup on a piece of scrap, I can complete the mortises in a couple of passes.

I used dowels to align and register the edge-glued top joints. I marked the location of the butterfly keys first, so I didn't end up with a dowel in the way later on. To give the top a light, thin appearance without compromising its strength, I tapered the underside of the top at the edge. I used a tall auxiliary fence clamped to the tablesaw's rip fence with the blade fully raised and tilted away from the fence at about 5°. The fence is positioned about ⅝ in. away from the blade, and the top is run through the saw on edge. A featherboard helps hold the top against the fence.

Tenoned, mortised and tapered legs

There are four steps in making the simple, tapered legs: sizing the stock, cutting the tenons, cutting the mortises and tapering the inside faces. Cutting the joints is much easier while the stock is still square. Leave the leg stock slightly long, so there will be an extra ¹⁄₁₆ in. or so of the tenon protruding through the top. Although the tenon will be sanded or planed flush later, the result is a cleaner finished joint.

To prepare a tenon for a wedge, I drill a hole just above the tenon's shoulder, so the wedge won't split the leg. Then I bandsaw a

Coffee table

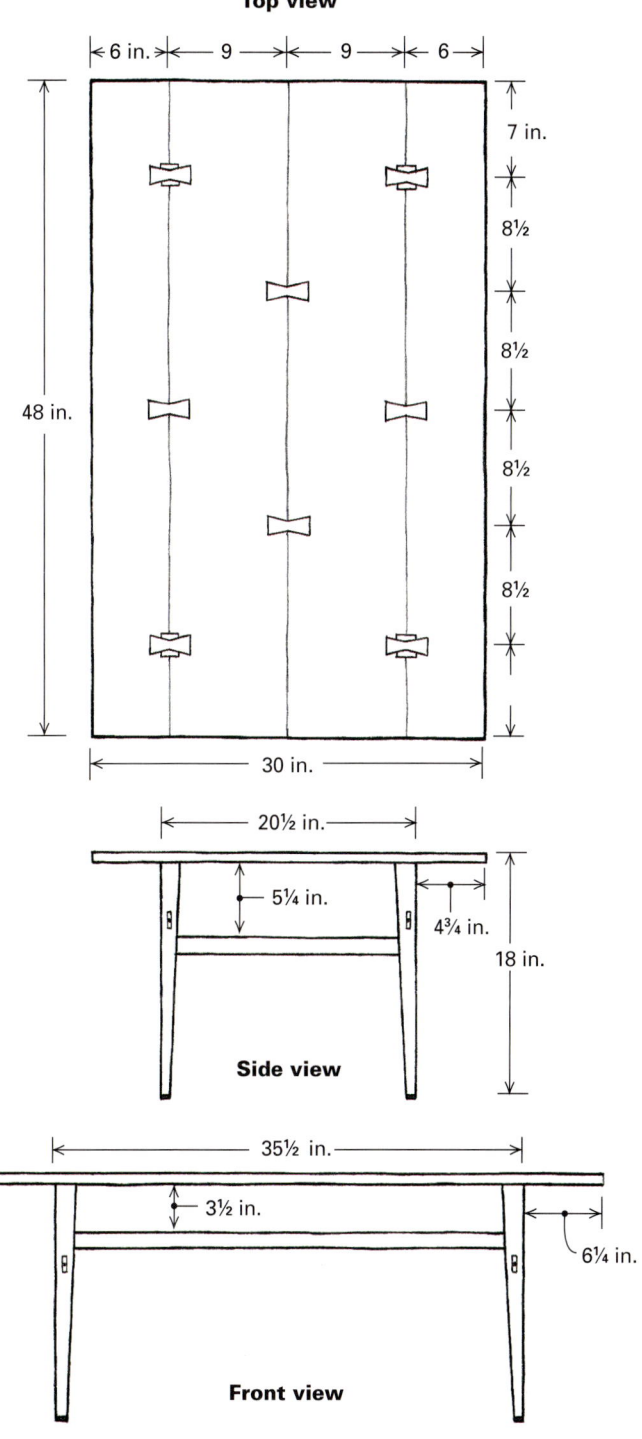

Top view

6 in. · 9 · 9 · 6

48 in.

7 in.

8½

8½

8½

8½

30 in.

20½ in.

5¼ in.

4¾ in.

18 in.

Side view

35½ in.

3½ in.

6¼ in.

Front view

A low coffee table makes the most of wildly figured wood. Mortises are cut in the top before glue-up.

Tabletop mortises ___

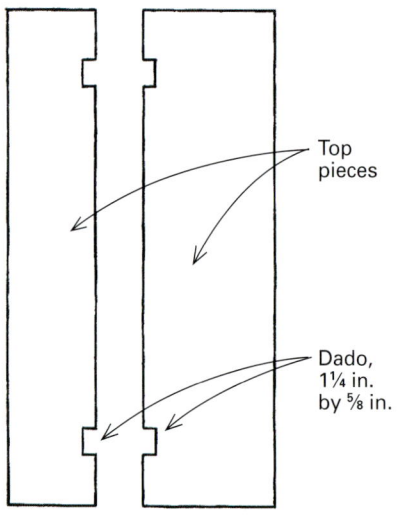

Top pieces

Dado, 1¼ in. by ⅝ in.

I taper the legs on the tablesaw using a shop-built jig, a rectangular piece of plywood cut to an L-shape. After double-checking that I'm tapering the inside faces of the legs, I run the jig along the fence of the tablesaw with the leg snugly seated in the jig. The offcuts are handy for cutting the stretcher shoulders to the angle of the legs.

I rescued some small scraps of ebony for the feet. The ¼-in.-thick ebony wears like iron and visually punctuates the ends of the tapered legs. I cut and glue the foot to the bottom of the leg and then countersink a screw for good measure.

Lay out stretchers from the legs

I measure and mark the stretchers by dry-fitting the legs into the top and clamping the stretcher in position at the correct height against the back of the legs. I leave a little extra length at both ends, so the tenons will protrude through the legs and can be sanded flush later. I use the tapered, inside edge of the leg as a guide to scribe the shoulder line on the stretcher.

To cut the tenon with an angled shoulder, I use a tenoning jig on the tablesaw. Instead of clamping the stretcher in a vertical position, I back it up with an offcut from tapering the legs. This ensures the angle of the shoulder will match the angle of the tapered leg. As before, I clean up, pare and fit the tenons and then drill and kerf them for wedges.

Assemble the frame in two steps

Before assembling the table, I make plenty of wedges from stock that's strong, straight grained and contrasting in color to accent the joint. I also scrape and sand all the parts. Then I glue up two sets of legs to the long stretchers only. After applying glue to the leg-stretcher joints, I fit the joints firmly and set them with a wedge. Then, immediately, I set the assembly into the tabletop (without glue). This holds everything in the correct position.

After the glue has cured, I repeat the procedure with the shorter end stretchers. When these are dry, I glue and wedge the leg/stretcher assembly to the top. I use the top wedges to keep the leg tenons tight in the top until the butterfly keys are finally

kerf down the tenon to the hole. Remember to orient the leg wedges so that they run perpendicular to the grain of the tabletop, not with it.

Before cutting the mortises for the stretchers, I mark each leg so I know where it belongs on the table and which faces are on the outside. Then I lay out the mortises on all the legs. I cut the mortises on a slot mortiser, but a router, drill press or mallet and chisel will work equally well.

The butterfly keys

Butterfly-mortise jig, made of plywood, is cut to shape and glued back together.

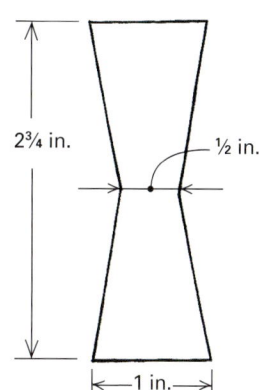

2¾ in.

½ in.

1 in.

Mortises on the tablesaw—The tabletop mortises are cut with a dado blade and a crosscut sled. Mating boards are clamped face to face against the sled's fence.

put into place. When the glue is fully cured, I sand the tenons and wedges flush with the legs and the top.

A jig simplifies the butterfly keys

When making multiple, identical butterfly joints, I like to cut all the mortises with a jig first and then fit the butterflies to the mortises. I make the butterflies with a slight taper on the sides, which helps ensure a tight fit and keeps the leg tenons tight in the top.

The butterfly jig is a rectangular piece of ¾-in.-thick plywood cut into three sections. I cut the center section with a chop saw to shape the butterfly (see the top photo). The pieces are glued back together, and centerlines are drawn to help with registration.

I lay out the centerlines for all the butterfly locations on the tabletop. Long layout lines make it easier to align the jig on the

Align butterfly-mortising jig with layout lines. The rounded corners left by the router bit in the butterfly mortises are cleaned out with a chisel.

tabletop (see the photo above). After clamping the jig securely in place, I rout the mortises with a flush-trimming, bearing-guided bit to a depth of about $7/16$ in. To complete the mortises, I clean up the corners with a chisel. I mill the butterfly stock to $1/2$ in. thick and use the mortising jig to mark out the butterflies. After I bandsaw them to shape, I fit each butterfly, carving a slight taper on the sides. Each butterfly and its corresponding mortise are numbered.

I glue and clamp the butterflies in place, spreading the glue completely, but sparingly, on the taper and on the bottom of the butterfly. I use deep-throated clamps and waxed blocks between joint and clamp. The blocks spread the clamp pressure over the whole butterfly and protect it from damage; the wax keeps the block from being glued to the top. The center butterflies can be tapped into place with a hammer and a block of wood while supporting the top from below. Or they can be clamped with

battens above and below the table with clamps at either side.

When the glue has dried, I use a sharp jack plane to level the protruding butterflies with the tabletop. Then I sand the top starting with 120-grit sandpaper, progressing up to 320-grit.

Finish up with oil and varnish

My favorite finish is a progressive buildup of four or five coats, starting with a straight oil finish, such as Watco. With each successive coat, I add a little semigloss varnish and mineral spirits in equal parts until the mix consists of approximately one-third of each ingredient.

This finish gives a soft, lustrous surface with better wear resistance than straight oil. After the final coat is dry, I wax and lightly buff the entire piece with #0000 steel wool and then polish with a soft cloth.

Wedge tenons and add butterfly keys

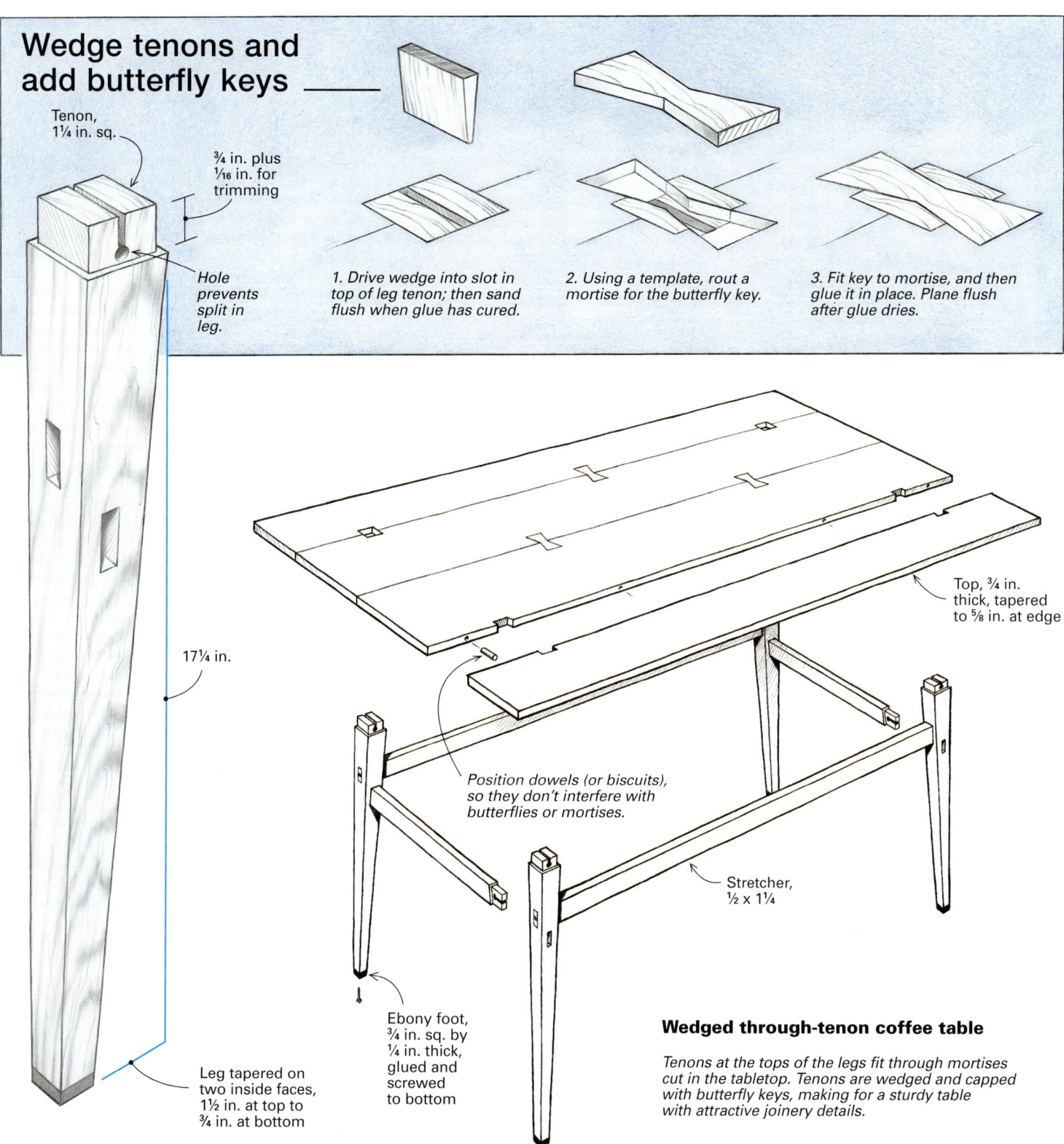

Tenon, 1¼ in. sq.

¾ in. plus 1/16 in. for trimming

Hole prevents split in leg.

1. Drive wedge into slot in top of leg tenon; then sand flush when glue has cured.

2. Using a template, rout a mortise for the butterfly key.

3. Fit key to mortise, and then glue it in place. Plane flush after glue dries.

17¼ in.

Leg tapered on two inside faces, 1½ in. at top to ¾ in. at bottom

Position dowels (or biscuits), so they don't interfere with butterflies or mortises.

Top, ¾ in. thick, tapered to ⅝ in. at edge

Stretcher, ½ x 1¼

Ebony foot, ¾ in. sq. by ¼ in. thick, glued and screwed to bottom

Wedged through-tenon coffee table

Tenons at the tops of the legs fit through mortises cut in the tabletop. Tenons are wedged and capped with butterfly keys, making for a sturdy table with attractive joinery details.

CURVED TABLE APRONS

by Bruce Peterson

Curved apron is veneered plywood. The author laminated layers of bending plywood capped by veneer around a circular form to make the apron for this table.

$\mathbf{A}$s a furniture builder, I'm always looking for production methods that save time but don't sacrifice quality. A good example is a series of veneered tables with circular aprons that I build to sell through galleries. The joinery is simple, so I can concentrate on the details: veneer-matching, shaping, inlaying and finishing. I have a vacuum bag, which speeds up the veneer work considerably, and I use jigs to taper the legs and to cut the joinery that connects the legs to the apron. The challenge was figuring out how to make strong and stable round aprons quickly.

Initially, I considered the more traditional methods of forming a curve out of solid wood. But those methods are neither easy nor economical. Steam-bending requires equipment and set-up time. Laminating and bricklaying solid wood involve lots of cutting, fitting and clamping.

What I needed was a faster, less-expensive way to form a curved apron. I experimented with laminating strips of

$^3/_8$-in. bending plywood around a circular mold, or form. With some refinement, I could make a small table apron, ready for veneer, in just a few hours. And this construction is more stable and quite a bit lighter than a solid-wood apron.

The trick to this process is the bending plywood I use to make the circular form and the table apron (see the bottom photo on the facing page). The plywood can be bent into fairly tight curves, but it will only bend along one axis. The two most common types are Wiggle Wood (also called Wacky Wood or Bendy Board) and Italian bending poplar. Wiggle Wood is available in $^1/_4$-in. and $^3/_8$-in. thicknesses. Italian bending plywood is 3mm thick (just under $^1/_8$ in.). Both come in 4x8 sheets. Large lumberyards carry one or both varieties. I used $^3/_8$-in. Wiggle Wood for my table aprons.

Designing the table and the building forms

I use two wooden forms (see the photo on p. 34) to make my plywood aprons: one is for a three-layer core and the other for a veneered outer layer that's glued to the core. The outer "skin" is made in quadrants that fit the spaces between the four legs. I veneer these arc sections in my vacuum press. The two forms shown in the drawings on p. 32 are the keys to getting tightly glued layers in the apron.

To size the forms, make a full-scale, top-view drawing of your table. From this drawing, you can get the diameters and the arc lengths you'll need. I take scraps of the plywood, bend them in a curve and set them on edge right over the drawing so that I can gauge and mark the thicknesses of the apron layers.

The end table I made is $20^1/_2$ in. dia. (see the photo above). Its four legs are made from $1^7/_8$-in. cherry. The table's plywood apron is $2^1/_4$ in. wide, and the top, made from $1^1/_8$-in. medium-density fiberboard (MDF), is veneered with book-matched Carpathian elm burl.

A form for the inner core

The form for the apron's three-layer core is a wheel of bending plywood reinforced with $^3/_4$-in. plywood (see the photo above). The form's diameter is just under eight thicknesses of bending plywood less than the outside-to-outside dimension of the table apron. To be exact, figure in the two thicknesses of veneer (usually $^1/_{28}$ in. each), as well.

To make the top and bottom of the form, cut two circles of $^3/_4$-in. plywood.

Bendable plywood— The author uses Wiggle Wood to make circular table aprons. The wood comes in 4x8 sheets, either $^1/_4$ in. or $^3/_8$ in. thick.

Bending forms _____

Bending forms

To determine the exact shape of the two forms used to make circular aprons, the author starts with a line representing the diameter of the finished apron (right). The outside edge of the circular form for the apron's core is found by subtracting four layers of plywood plus the veneer.

The radius of the form used to make the apron's outer skin is one layer of plywood and one thickness of veneer less than the apron's finished diameter.

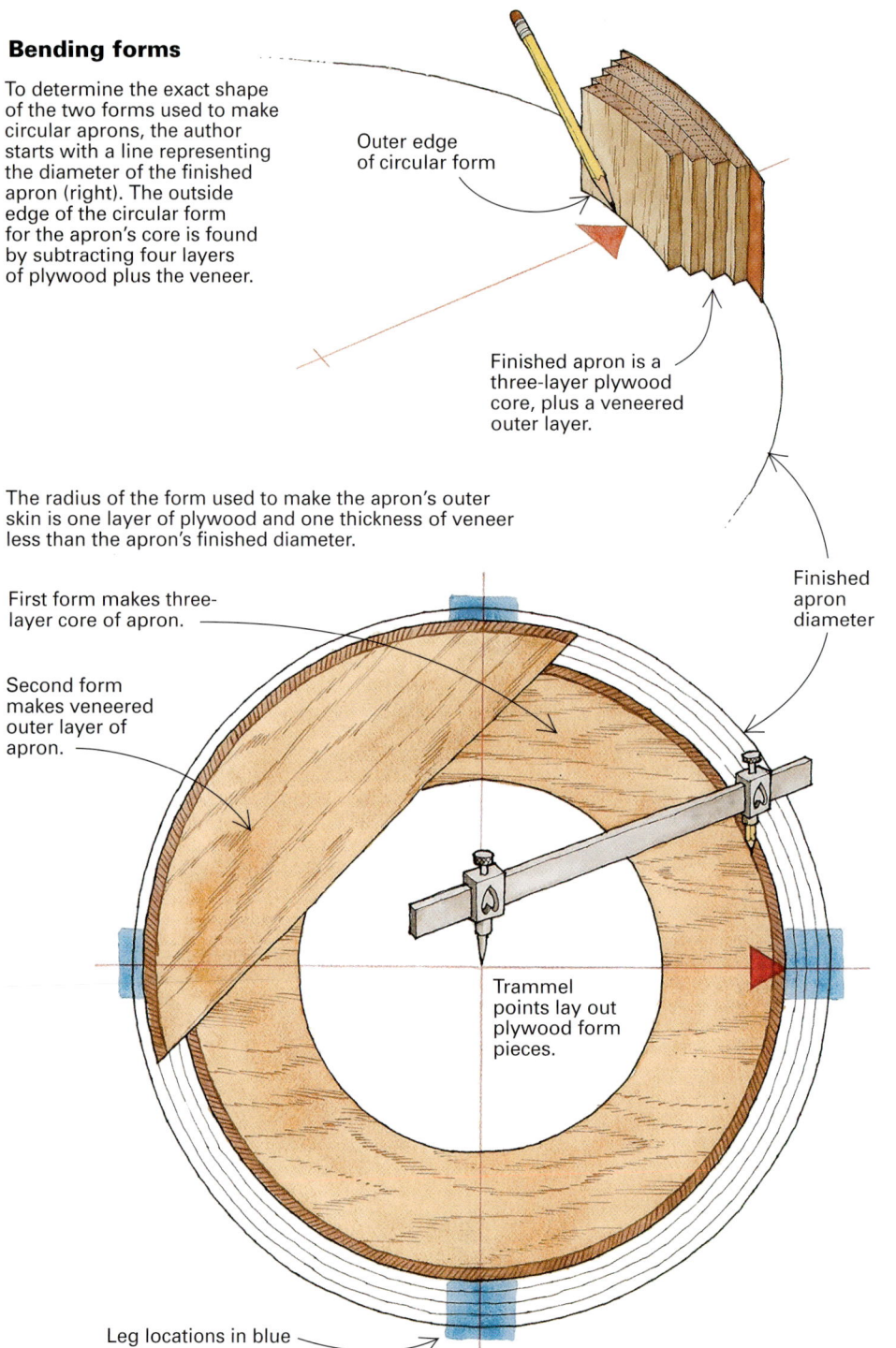

Outer edge
of circular form

Finished apron is a three-layer plywood core, plus a veneered outer layer.

Finished apron diameter

First form makes three-layer core of apron.

Second form makes veneered outer layer of apron.

Trammel points lay out plywood form pieces.

Leg locations in blue

They should be two thicknesses of bending ply less in diameter than the inside of the finished apron (see the bottom drawing on the facing page). Cut out the centers of the top and bottom so they're hollow, like tires.

With the top aligned over the bottom, insert, glue and nail six or eight plywood pieces between them. The pieces, which are higher than the apron width, resemble the spokes in a water wheel. Glue and tack (I used staples) a layer of bending plywood around the wheel.

A form for the outer, veneered skin

The form for the outer, veneered layer of the apron is an arc that's slightly longer than a quarter of the table-apron core. The radius of the form is the outside radius of the apron less one layer of bending plywood and the thickness of the veneer.

This form must be strong to withstand the pressure of the vacuum press. It should be about 18 in. from end to end so you will have enough room to glue four to six quarter sections at a time. Having one or two extra quarters is a good idea in case you ruin one of them during glue-up. And the extras can speed things up if you are doing a production run. To make the form, wrap and fasten a layer of bending ply over ribs of $^3/_4$-in. plywood that are attached to a plywood baseplate, as shown in the photo on the facing page.

If you plan to use hide glue and a veneer hammer or yellow glue and an iron to attach the veneer to the apron, you do not need to build this second form. You would laminate four layers of plywood (instead of three) over the first form. I like using a second form; in the vacuum press, it produces veneered quadrants that are bent in rigid arcs, ready to be attached to the core. I use epoxy for veneering because it makes a good bond and gives good working time. Also, epoxy reduces the cracking, lifting and chipping that can occur on the edges of delicate veneers.

Cutting and gluing up the apron

Cut the plywood for the apron layers in strips that are $^1/_8$ in. over-width to allow for trimming. You'll need three strips for the inner core and a fourth for the veneered, outer layer. Wrap the innermost strip

Three layers of plywood are painted with thinned glue and then wrapped and clamped on the form.

around the core form, and mark the strip where the two ends butt. Cut the strip $^1/_4$ in. short of this length so that it can be drawn together tightly on the form. Tape the strip temporarily in place on the form.

In a similar manner, wrap the second layer around the first strip, and then tape it. Do the same thing with the third and fourth layers. If you measure these lengths now, you can cut strips for subsequent tables. Dry-assemble to make sure that all the layers compress nicely. Remove the layers from the form, and then cut the fourth strip in quarters.

I use yellow glue that's been thinned with water to about the consistency of light cream. Thinning the glue will allow the layers to slide past one another as they are clamped. I use an old paint brush to apply the glue to one side of the three core strips (see the photo above).

I clamp the layers together with two band clamps, making sure that the joints of the strips are staggered. After a few hours, I remove the clamps and trim and clean up the apron's edges. A jointer or stationary belt sander works well for this.

While the aprons are drying, I veneer the quarter-section pieces that make up the

Using the forms

Three layers of ³⁄₈-in. bending plywood are glued to the circular plywood form with a band clamp to create the apron's inner core (at right and in the photo below). Joints should be staggered.

Core of bending plywood

Leg locations in blue

Leave ¼-in. space.

Band clamp

Veneer is applied to the last layer of plywood on a second form and then glued to the core (photo below). Filler blocks inserted in gaps between pieces help keep the core rigid during glue-up.

Filler block at ends of plywood

Veneer over bending plywood

fourth layer of the apron in a vacuum press. Once the veneered sections are removed from the press, I glue and clamp them to the core with band clamps. I like to fill in the voids between sections by gluing in apron and veneer scraps. The fillers don't have to look pretty because they'll be cut out for the leg sockets. But having a rigid, continuous circumference helps ensure accurate cuts.

I also plug any voids in the three inner layers. This gives the apron a cleaner look when viewed from below.

Joining the legs and the top to the apron

To join the legs to the apron, I use simple, but strong, half-lap joints reinforced with screws. This joinery allows the attachment of many different leg styles, and it is easy to do. Shape the legs after the joinery is cut, so you're working with stock that has straight sides and square corners. To determine where to lay out the leg sockets on the apron, return to your drawing. I like to place the apron directly on the diagram and transfer the leg locations to both the top and bottom of the apron.

Use a tablesaw to cut the limits of the dadoes for the half-lap joints in the apron. The depth of the dadoes is one-half the thickness of the apron. A scrap of MDF cut in the arc of the apron and clamped to the miter gauge makes a handy jig that helps steady the cut (see the top right photo).

Take a practice cut somewhere inside your marks to make sure that the blade cuts square to the apron surface. Then carefully line up the apron marks, and make your cuts. Although the cut is not too deep, it's a good idea to clamp the work securely to the jig in case the piece should kick back.

Next use a bandsaw to remove the waste between the sawcuts (see the bottom right photo). Test-fit the legs into each dado. Now rabbet the upper backs of the legs so that they will slip into the apron.

The depth of these recesses determines how much the leg protrudes from the outside of the apron. I like the leg to be about 1/4 in. proud. Shape the legs to their final form, and then glue them into place. Drive two screws in from the back of the apron to reinforce the joint.

Forming the leg sockets—The author starts on a tablesaw, using a miter-gauge jig to cut the ends of a half-lap joint for each leg (above). A bandsaw removes the rest of the waste (below).

TWO

Carcase and Boxes

A mitered box with edges that line up perfectly? As the stereotypical Maine farmer would say, "You can't get there from here." The number of commercial miter jigs available says something about how difficult this particular joint is to get right. But here's a woodworker with an almost foolproof solution: tape. This illustrates a cardinal rule of woodworking: The best solutions are rarely complex, and it's a sure sign you're missing something when you've put 30 hours into a jig that still doesn't work right. Just remember that simple tape gets you perfect miters, so stop looking above your head and start looking right in front of you.

Simplicity can even escape a generation of woodworkers. Steve Latta questioned the gospel of putting a reinforcing spline into a plywood miter joint. Everybody knows that gluing a simple miter joint doesn't make it strong enough. There just isn't enough glue surface, right? But Latta tried it, and found that glued plywood miter joints were perfectly strong. With that simplification he has since saved a lot of time and trouble without sacrificing quality.

In the same vein, finger joints are another bugbear to get right. Traditional methods leave much to be desired with complex measuring and spacing problems. Jack Danilchak has pared away all the confusion and offers a simple table-saw jig and some strategies to make the job as straightforward as it can be. He indeed makes the work look easy, as all good woodworkers do. Follow the advice in this section, and you might duplicate it.

Sometimes, there just isn't a good way to do something quickly, but there is always a good way to do it. Malcolm Vaughn did not want to sacrifice quality to make his dresser easier to build. He did find a very simple bandsaw jig and other strategies to ensure accuracy and consistency. And when you attain those two, you always save time.

STRONG, NO CLAMP-UP CORNER JOINTS

by Steve Latta

A good part of my early woodworking career was spent making cheap, lacquered medium-density fiberboard (MDF) furniture. My co-workers and I called it curb furniture because of its inevitable resting place. Despite the lack of inspiration or style, working in that shop taught me a valuable skill: how to make foolproof mitered corner joints. All case work was done this way because we had to hide the ugly edges of MDF, which telegraph through paint.

Eleven years and three shops later, I now spend my days building reproduction 18th-century American furniture. Although this job calls for a lot of traditional joinery—dovetail and mortise and tenon—the mitering technique used to join slabs of MDF has a place here, too. It works on solid stock and is handsome and durable.

When mitering large stock on a tablesaw, most woodworkers use a traditional rip-cut method: One edge of the workpiece rides along the rip fence, and the other edge is mitered by the tilted blade.

There are problems with this method. Many tablesaws have a limited capacity between the fence and blade. Also, tilting your blade throws off the reading on the rip-fence scale. Safety is a concern, too. When mitering a wide piece, it's nerve-wracking to try to keep your eyes on the fence and sawblade at the same time. At the very least, stock cut this way is prone to minor imperfections unless you own a sliding-table attachment.

With my method, you first rip and crosscut all stock to finished dimensions, with square edges. Next cut any internal grooves or slots your project may require. Miters are cut with the blade buried in scrap stock clamped onto the rip fence. I should stress that although I've found this method to be perfectly safe, it's unconventional. My auxiliary fence and hold-down minimize the chance of the offcut kicking back. But you should always stand to the left of the blade, just in case. Most of the time, the offcut just rattles around harmlessly between the blade

Uses for mitered case work

These mitered corner joints are surprisingly strong, and they have many applications. They are appropriate for everything from basic boxes and bookshelves to fine furniture. You can use hardwoods or sheet goods or a combination as long as you avoid large areas of cross-grain with solid stock.

- **Matching grain:** You can match grain between a case side and the face frame if the stock is cut from the same board.

- **Speaker cabinets:** Leave one face open, and cover the exposed edges with strips of hardwood or iron-on edge-banding.

- **Plant stands:** Miter all six sides for a strong box, and finish it with something durable such as lacquer or urethane.

- **Bookcases:** Before joining the cases, drill holes for shelf pins. Or cut dadoes or biscuit slots to hold fixed shelves.

Tablesaw technique is key to perfect miters

Miter all sides of the stock. The miter cuts are made by pushing dimensioned stock along an auxiliary fence fitted with a hold-down covering the blade and a recess for the offcut. The blade is partly buried in the auxiliary fence.

How much to cut. The miter should not reduce the width of the workpiece, which is cut to finished dimensions first.

Tablesaw jig for cutting miters _____

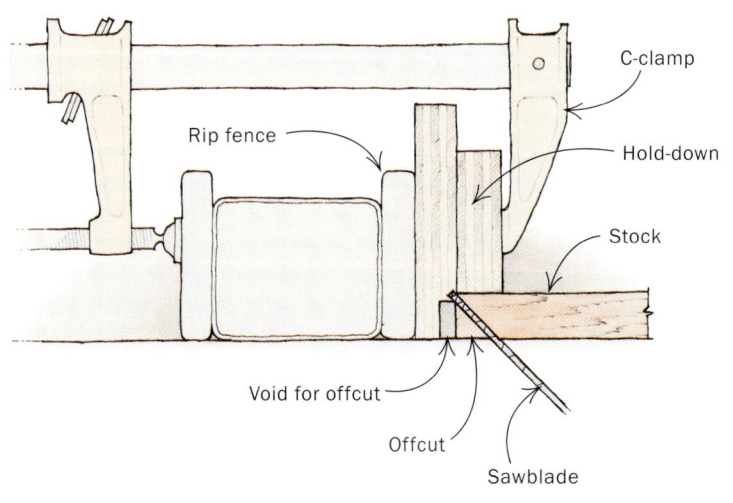

Rip fence

C-clamp

Hold-down

Stock

Void for offcut

Offcut

Sawblade

Tape the outside seams of the case. Position the panels of the case flush with each other, and pull them tight with strips of clear packing tape. Then spread tape along each joint.

and fence until the next piece of stock pushes it through. Alternatively, shut off the saw,
and between cuts, move the offcut out of the
way after the blade stops spinning. Also, buy
or make a zero-clearance throat-plate insert
for your tablesaw for added safety.

Make the auxiliary fence, and adjust the blade

There are two parts to my auxiliary fence
setup, and both can be made of $^3/_4$-in. stock,
solid wood or sheet goods. First cut a piece
of scrap about 3 in. wide and roughly the
length of your rip fence. Then cut a rabbet,
about $^1/_4$ in. deep, into this piece. Start with
a rabbet about $^1/_{16}$ in. narrower than the
thickness of the stock being mitered, and
make sure that's enough room for the offcut.
The offcut must be able to float freely in
this space until the next cut pushes it
through or until the saw coasts to a stop.

Cut another piece of scrap, about $1^1/_2$ in.
to 2 in. wide by 12 in. to 16 in. long for the
hold-down. Clamp both pieces to the rip
fence. Place a workpiece under the hold-
down when making adjustments. Stock
should slide through with only the slightest
trace of resistance.

The relationship between the fence and
blade is critical for precise, safe cuts. Adjust

the blade (tilted at 45°) and rip fence until
the blade's teeth are aimed directly at, but
not touching, the outside corner of the rabbet. Then turn on the saw, and slowly raise
the blade into the auxiliary fence, only about
$^1/_8$ in. The outside face of the blade, where it
enters the auxiliary fence, should be as high
as the stock being cut is thick. That way,
when cutting the miter, the outside dimensions of the stock remain constant. Cut a
piece of scrap from the same batch of stock
to check your settings (see the bottom photo
on p. 40).

Be sure all your stock is the same thickness

Because the auxiliary fence is rabbeted, your
stock is riding on only a small portion of the
fence. Be sure all the stock is the same
thickness. Remember: Sheets of plywood
may vary in thickness, so measure all your
stock before beginning.

When you're ready to miter, keep your
body to the left of the blade, out of the path
of potential harm (see the top photo on
p. 40). It's also a good idea to have an on/off
switch you can reach without having to step
into the kickback zone. Most of the time,
cutoffs will just rattle and float back. Offcuts
can be pushed through the blade with suc-

cessive passes of stock. Or turn off the saw between cuts, and when the blade stops spinning, remove the offcut.

With this method, I've mitered components as large as 36 in. by 84 in. and as small as 12 in. Don't put anything against your rip fence that's less than a foot long.

Forget about splines— miters go together with glue

I was taught that miters require slots for reinforcing splines, and that's how I built them for many years. Inserting a long spline into a long groove that is tacky with rapidly drying glue can give you fits. Sometimes the spline just jams up. Several years ago, while employed at the curb-furniture shop, I realized a strong, spline-free miter would make my job easier.

The idea of abandoning splines was heresy. Nonetheless, I found a few willing heretics, and we conspired to build and test a spline-free cube about 18 in. sq. After gluing it up and letting it cure, we proceeded to abuse it. We repeatedly pitched it off a plywood rack to the concrete floor below, a distance of about 12 ft. We beat it with hammers. We stood on it. The cube remained intact; its corners were blunted, but the joints held fast.

For a strong mitered corner, you need perfectly flat mating surfaces, a tight clamp-up and a lot of yellow glue. Glue-up will be messy, but you don't want to starve the joint, especially with glue-hungry plywood. Solid stock requires less glue.

After mitering the stock, lay it down on a large workbench. A sheet of MDF or plywood makes a good work surface. Arrange the four sides in sequence, outside face up, and tape the panels together along the seams, using clear packing tape (see the photo on p. 41). The tape acts as a hinge when you fold the four sides into a box. Then flip the case over, and mask off the inside corners. Make sure you don't tape the miter. The tape keeps the glue squeeze-out off the wood. If you're building a plant stand or something where the insides won't be seen, skip this step.

Make sure the corners are flush. Last, tape the top and bottom pieces in place.

Run a generous bead of glue along all the mitered surfaces, and spread it out with a brush. When I'm using plywood, I add a second coating of glue. Then fold the box into shape, and tape the last corner (see the photo above). Finish up by gluing and taping the top and bottom pieces. If your miters are all 45°, the box will align itself perfectly square. Let the glue set for about an hour or so, then rip off the tape, and scrape off any remaining squeeze-out using a cabinet scraper. When the glue has cured, burnish the sharp corners of the box using the wooden handle of a chisel, then sand lightly.

FINGER-JOINING SMALL BOXES

by Jack Danilchak

Gang-cutting box sides speeds the work. The author clamps all four sides together and makes multiple kerf-width passes using a guide pin to index each successive pass.

Finger-joining jig

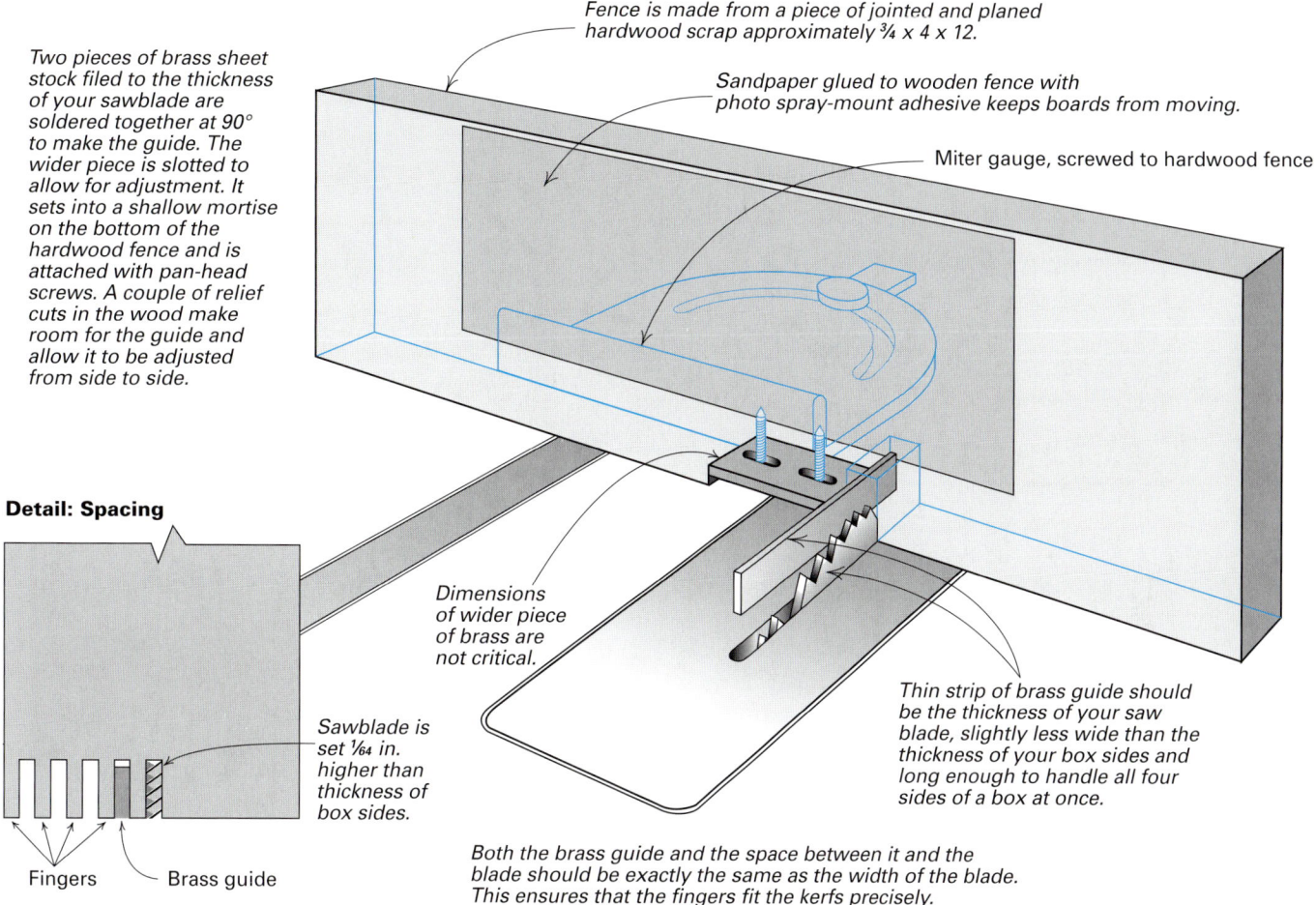

Fence is made from a piece of jointed and planed hardwood scrap approximately ¾ x 4 x 12.

Sandpaper glued to wooden fence with photo spray-mount adhesive keeps boards from moving.

Miter gauge, screwed to hardwood fence

Two pieces of brass sheet stock filed to the thickness of your sawblade are soldered together at 90° to make the guide. The wider piece is slotted to allow for adjustment. It sets into a shallow mortise on the bottom of the hardwood fence and is attached with pan-head screws. A couple of relief cuts in the wood make room for the guide and allow it to be adjusted from side to side.

Detail: Spacing

Dimensions of wider piece of brass are not critical.

Sawblade is set ¹⁄₆₄ in. higher than thickness of box sides.

Thin strip of brass guide should be the thickness of your saw blade, slightly less wide than the thickness of your box sides and long enough to handle all four sides of a box at once.

Fingers   Brass guide

Both the brass guide and the space between it and the blade should be exactly the same as the width of the blade. This ensures that the fingers fit the kerfs precisely.

I learned feather jointing from Max, a sawyer friend whose sawmill is in the mountains near Uniontown, Pa. A feather joint is a smaller version of a finger or box joint. Each finger is only as wide as the kerf of your tablesaw blade, which gives the joint a delicate look. But the cumulative surface area of the joint is great, making it quite strong. Because of the diminutive size of the individual fingers, it's a joint best suited to small boxes and drawers (see the bottom photo on the facing page).

Although it looks like it would be difficult because of the fineness of the fingers, feather jointing is actually quite simple. That's because you cut both sides of each joint at the same time, rather than cutting

one half and then matching the second half to the first. The crux of this joint is getting the jig right in the first place. Once you've got your jig fine-tuned, perfect joinery is all but guaranteed.

Making the jig

My feather-jointing jig mounts on a tablesaw miter gauge, and consists of a short piece of hardwood and a couple of pieces of brass sheet stock, soldered together and screwed to the bottom of the piece of hardwood to form a guide (see the drawing above). The critical aspect of building this jig is getting the spacing right, so that the joint will go together just right. The way to get this spacing is to make the blade, guide

Arranging box sides for gang-cutting finger joints _____

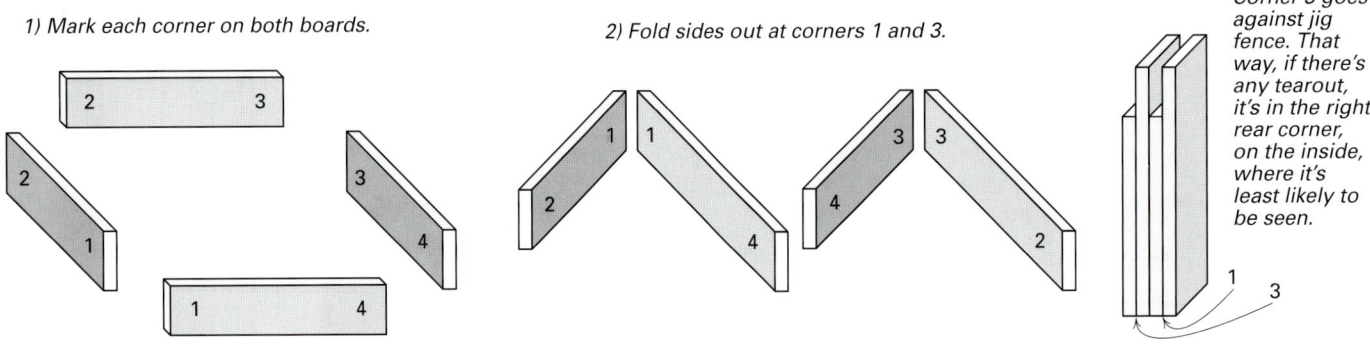

1) Mark each corner on both boards.

2) Fold sides out at corners 1 and 3.

3) Stack together, corners 1 and 3 down and flush.

Corner 3 goes against jig fence. That way, if there's any tearout, it's in the right rear corner, on the inside, where it's least likely to be seen.

and space between the two exactly the same. That way kerfs and fingers are exactly the same width.

The first thing you have to do is get the blade and guide to the same thickness. The best way of doing this is to buy brass stock thicker than the blade you intend to use for feather-jointing, and then file and sand the brass until it's exactly as thick as the blade.

With my brass stock to thickness, I hacksawed the two pieces to size, soldered them together and ground them smooth. I drilled two series of adjacent holes across the bottom of the wider piece of brass, and then turned the holes into a pair of slots with a needle file.

I mortised the bottom of a piece of hardwood for the wider piece of brass and made a few kerfs into the board to make space for the narrow piece of brass (see the drawing on p. 45). Then I screwed the guide to the piece of hardwood, screwed the jig to my miter gauge so the thin brass guide strip was about a blade's width from the blade and made a series of test-cuts into two $^5/_{16}$-in. boards. I tweaked the position of the brass guide until I got a snug fit with the two test boards and then tightened down the panhead screws that hold the guide in place.

Feather-jointing the box sides

The construction of the box begins with the sides. I rip the side stock about $^1/_4$ in. wider than I want it. This allows me to joint stock off the tops of two sides to get the tops even and then to rip all four sides down to final width. The tops of my boxes add about $^3/_8$ in. to the height of the box, so I account for this when I'm figuring the width I rip the sides to—usually $2^1/_4$ in.

I arrange the sides of the box as they will be when the box is assembled, with the grain wrapping all the way around, and chalk a number onto both boards that make up each corner, 1 through 4. Then I fold out the two sides that make up corner 1 and the two sides that make up corner 3, so that the outside faces of the box are facing each other (see the drawing above). I clamp the stack together with a small handscrew or a couple of little bar clamps, making sure the top edges of the box sides and corners 1 and 3 are flush. Then I butt the stack up against the hardwood jig fence, with corner 3 against the fence and the tops of the box sides against the brass guide.

My tablesaw blade is set $^1/_{64}$ in. higher than the thickness of the box sides, so that when the box is assembled the fingers will be slightly long. It's easier to sand off the pins than to take all the whole box sides down to meet the fingers because the kerfs weren't taken deep enough. I feather-joint

Push box for handling small parts on the tablesaw _____

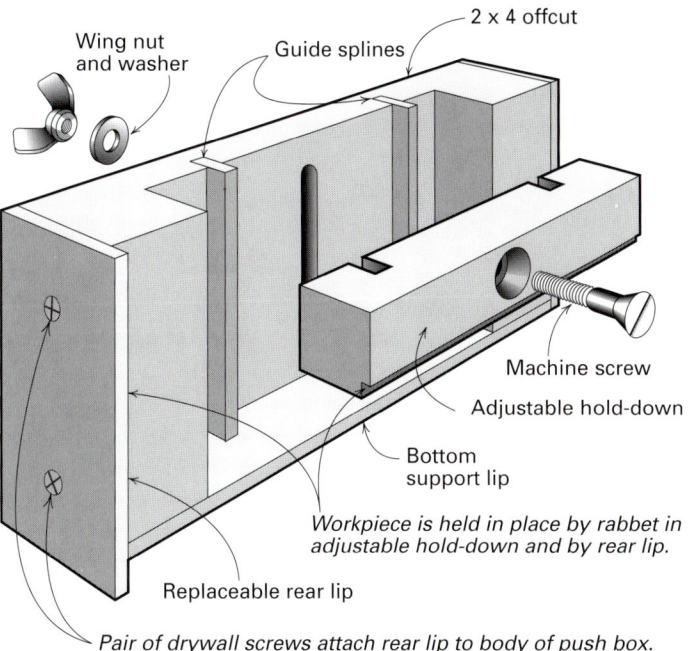

Wing nut and washer

Guide splines

2 x 4 offcut

Machine screw

Adjustable hold-down

Bottom support lip

Workpiece is held in place by rabbet in adjustable hold-down and by rear lip.

Replaceable rear lip

Pair of drywall screws attach rear lip to body of push box.

from the outfeed side of my saw so I can see what I'm doing as I'm pulling the box sides through the blade. It's a small saw, a model-maker's saw actually, so I don't have to reach very far, and in addition to being able to see better from the outfeed side of the table, I also feel like I have more control pulling the stock into the blade than I would pushing it. On a standard-size tablesaw, though, you'll probably just want to work slowly and carefully from the infeed side of the table, so you're not stretching too far.

I make the first cut with the top edge of the box sides up against the brass guide. After that I make each subsequent cut by moving the box sides so the kerf I've just made is over the guide (see the top photo on p. 44). I'm careful to feed the wood smoothly through the blade so as not to cause any tear-out.

I dry-assemble the sides once I'm done feather-jointing. Two of the box's sides are high (whether it's front and back or the two sides depends on how you've assembled them), so I mark the high sides and run

them over my little 4-in. jointer, though you could also do it with a handplane. Then, with the tops of all four sides even I set the tablesaw fence to about $2^{1}/_{4}$ in. and rip the sides to final width. I say "about $2^{1}/_{4}$ in." because, with fingers of adjacent sides alternating, if I ripped to exactly $2^{1}/_{4}$ in. there's a good chance I'd end up with a paper thin finger. Instead, I try to split a finger dead-center, so they're equally thick on either side of the corner.

Bottoms and tops

These boxes consist of ten parts: four sides, a bottom panel, and a top made of four frame members and a floating, raised panel. The top is not the lid, though. I glue the top to the sides after it's assembled, let the glue set, and then separate lid from box a little bit further down than where I glued on the top. This gives the lid an internal lip, a detail that just makes the box a bit nicer. But I'm getting ahead of myself.

Clamping jig ensures square boxes—Reversed hand screws inside a perfectly square box make clamping the author's boxes easy. Lines marked on the bottom of the clamping box allow him to check for square.

Cut small parts accurately and keep your fingers out of danger by using an adjustable push box. This jig exerts downward and lateral pressure to keep the workpiece flush against table and fence.

After reassembling the box sides, I set them on an already smoothed and thick-nessed bottom panel, usually of pine or another inexpensive secondary wood. I pen-cil around the inside of the box to mark the inside of the bottom-panel rabbet. I cut the rabbets around the perimeter of the bottom panel with a dado set on my radial-arm saw. For the grooves around the bottom of the box sides, I used a 1/8-in. router bit in my table-mounted router, using stop blocks to prevent the groove from showing on the outside of the box. Then I disassemble the dry-fitted box sides, insert the bottom panel, apply glue to the fingers with an artist's brush and glue the sides together to form the box. I clamp the box up in a special clamping device I made just for these boxes. The clamping device consists of a perfectly square box with movable clamping blocks that are held in place with wing-nuts. For clamps I use handscrews that have had their wooden faces reversed to exert pressure as they move apart, rather than as they come together (see the top photo at left).

The top consists of five pieces: four frame members and a floating raised panel. For the frame, I rip 3/8-in. stock to about 1 1/2 in. and then miter the pieces on my radial-arm saw. I cut them just slightly overlength, so the frame extends past the box sides by 1/16 in. or so on all sides. Then I groove the frame members for the raised panel by running them over the tablesaw blade. They're small pieces, though, and after a couple of boxes I began to grow nervous about the proximity of my fingers to the blade. To deal with these small pieces, I made a push-box. It's kind of an adjustable, enveloping push-stick, that cradles the frame members while exert-ing both lateral and downward pressure (see the photo at left and the drawing on p. 47). This little jig keeps my fingers safe and my cuts consistent.

I made another jig to kerf the corners of the frame, and used a toggle clamp and caul to hold two frame members at a time in place (see the top photo on the facing page). Supports orient the frame members correct-ly at 45 degrees to the tablesaw's surface. I

Cut spline slots safely and precisely with simple jig. A toggle clamp and caul hold frame members in place while a pair of screwed supports position the frame members at exactly 45° to the saw table.

use splines made of the same wood to join the frame members at the corners, applying glue with an artist's brush again. I leave the top panel, into which I've routed an ogee profile, floating free.

Once the glue has cured on the top, I rabbet around the underside of the top frame to the width of the sides and $\frac{1}{16}$-in. deep, so that the top pops down into the sides for a good seal. I then glue the top to the box's sides. When this has cured, I sand off the $\frac{1}{16}$-in. excess I left around the perimeter of the top, and then finish the boxes before separating top from bottom or attaching hardware. I use one coat of an oil/urethane finish to seal the box, and then apply a few coats of paste wax.

To open the box, I kerf it all around, about $\frac{3}{4}$ in. down from the top edge of the top frame (see the photo at right) and about $\frac{1}{64}$ in. shy of going through the box sides, because I don't want the box to separate on the tablesaw. Then I come back and separate top from bottom with a utility knife. After cleaning up the edges of the box's top and bottom with sandpaper and a sanding block, the box is ready for hardware. I predrill, attach hinges and latch and call it a day.

Cutting open the box to make the top—Kerf $\frac{1}{64}$ in. shy of going through the sides, so the box won't come apart on the tablesaw. A utility knife finishes the job.

VISIBLE JOINERY MAKES A CHEST

by Malcolm Vaughan

Early in the design of a small chest of drawers, I decided to lean in the direction of Arts and Crafts. I wanted the four-drawer bureau to have clean lines and simple edge profiles (see the photo below). As a decorative feature, I decided to wedge the through-tenons on the ends of the drawer dividers with pear, which would contrast with the black walnut I chose for the chest's carcase. I also selected pear for the drawer sides and backs, so the contrast would likewise accentuate the drawers dovetail joinery (see the top photo on the facing page). Finally, I picked aromatic cedar for the drawer bottoms and the chest's back panel, which floats in a conventional frame.

Quite a few furnituremakers feel it's extravagant to use solid wood as drawer dividers. But in my chest, I wanted solid dividers, though I didn't cut them from prime timber. In the time it would take me to join and glue-up web frames, I was able to make solid dividers that not only serve as drawer runners but also act as dust boards. And solid dividers allowed me to accent the chest's joinery; I penetrated the two sides with pairs of through-tenons at the corners of each of the three dividers and the bottom. This meant I had to make and insert 64 wedges. To speed the job along and help ensure that each of the joints would look alike (see the top photo on the facing page), I came up with a jig to quickly bandsaw identical wedges. Before I tell you about the wedges, though, I'll describe how I built the rest of the bureau, including how I laid out and routed out each of its 32 slightly flared mortises.

Chest construction

To start any furniture project, I make a dimensioned sketch, a materials list and an order of operations, which usually saves me from cutting pieces the wrong size, gluing parts together too soon and wasting time. For the chest (see the drawing on p. 53), I cut, shaped and fit components and joinery in the following order:

Sides

Before I edge-jointed the boards for the sides, I tapered the stock's thickness using a carrier jig in my surface planer. Next I cut the sides to dimension and cleaned up all the surfaces. Then I cut dadoes to support the ends of the dividers, and I rabbeted the edge of the sides to retain the back. To mark out the dadoes, I lightly knifed their posi-

Subtle geometry in this chest of drawers built by Malcolm Vaughan accentuates both the wood and the form, reflecting the honesty in materials and manufacture that is the hallmark of the Arts-and-Crafts style. Vaughan boldly pierced the bureau's side with the through-tenon ends of the drawer dividers, contrasting black walnut tenons with pear wedges.

tions across both faces of the sides. This makes for accurate mortising later and eliminates tearout around the mortise edges.

Dividers

When I was cutting out the dividers and bottom, I double checked the ends for squareness across their width (if they're not square, subsequent fitting of the drawers is a nightmare). It's actually not a bad idea for a carcase to widen slightly toward the back, and many cabinetmakers build such an "inaccuracy" into their cases.

Bandsawing the tenons

After planing the dividers for a tight fit in the dadoes, I marked off each end for a double pair of tenons. Next I bandsawed the tenon cheeks using a sharp, fine-tooth blade. I guided the edge of each board along the rip fence, and I clamped a stop block to the table to keep from cutting too far. To remove the waste and establish the land between the tenons, I guided my router (fitted with a $\frac{1}{4}$-in. straight bit and a long fence) along the ends of each board. After routing, I cleaned up the corners with a chisel. Next I hand-sawed the dividers' front shoulders. Finally I went back to the bandsaw to cut slots in the tenons for the wedges, each time setting the rip fence to guide the cut.

Cutting the mortises

To mark out all the mortises, I slid the end of each divider into its corresponding dado, carefully aligning the rear edge with the edge of the rabbet, and then I scribed the locations in the dado using an awl. To mark the mortise locations on the outside face of the side, I again laid the divider in position against the side (close to one of my earlier-made lower dado lines) and nicked positions with my knife.

The real trick to get the wedges to fit uniformly is to flare both sides of each mortise the same amount ($\frac{1}{16}$ in.) toward the side's outer face (see the drawing detail on the facing page). To mark the flare, I first clamped a straightedge across the outside, close to the lower dado line. Then I took a short piece of stock the same thickness as what would be the flared tenon width, and laid it square to the straightedge. Centering

Tight through-tenons—The author gets uniform and snugly fitting through-tenons by driving the wedges into the tenon slots an equal amount. This requires all the wedges be identical and all the mortises be the same size. It also means the side walls of the mortises must be flared uniformly to correspond to the wedge angle.

Wedge-o-matic—Vaughan made a simple jig to bandsaw consistent wedges for 32 through-tenons. To use the jig, he first inserts a corner of a piece of pear (with its grain running across the width) into a notch in the jig's base. Then he slides the base along the fence to slice off a wedge.

this piece over each tenon location let me knife exactly to where the tenon would spread once it was wedged. Taking a few minutes to accurately mark out at this stage guaranteed that all the wedges would drive into the tenons at the same depth and thus appear uniform in width.

I wasted most of each mortise with a router fitted with a $\frac{1}{4}$-in. bit. While I was at it, I routed a mortise in each divider to house drawer stops (see the drawing on the facing page). Finally I chiseled squarely to the lines.

Dry-fitting and shaping

Next came the dry-fitting. I always enjoy this part because it lets me see, for the first time, the piece of furniture taking shape from what started out as a pile of rough-sawn boards. To hold the components in place as I checked the joints for proper fit, I made four sets of side cauls, which I bar-clamped across the width of the case near each row of mortises. The cauls, which have a slightly convex face, ensure that the dividers go fully into their dadoes; without the cauls, the center of the sides might bow outward.

After dismantling the chest, I slightly rounded the front edges of the sides with a plane, checking the profile against a cardboard template. Using an old *Fine Woodworking* "Quick tip," I smoothed the curves with a piece of sandpaper, which was wrapped around a half deck of playing cards. To create shallow feet at the corners, I used my spokeshave to shape and chamfer the bottom of the sides. Then masking off all the joints with tape, I finish-sanded and waxed the chest's inside faces, which would be much more difficult to do after glue-up.

Mass-producing wedges

To cut out the wedges, I returned to my trusty bandsaw to use a shopmade wedge-making jig. The bottom photo above shows how I inserted the corner of my $^3/_4$-in.-thick pear stock (with the grain running across its width) in a corner of the jig's medium-density fiberboard base. After slicing off each wedge, I flipped the wood over and repeated the cut until I piled up enough wedges for the job. Then I regathered my cauls and clamps, and I took a deep breath in preparation for gluing up the dividers into the sides.

Assembling the case

Initially, I was concerned that knocking in 64 wedges before the glue set up would be a desperate race against the clock. As it turned out, it didn't take long at all. If you're still worried about time, I suggest you use a two-part glue, and dip the wedges in the catalyst part just before you insert them.

Most woodworking textbooks rightly say that wedges should run across the grain and not with it. They also say to drill holes at the end of the tenon slots. Well, I didn't do either of those things on my chest, but I had no problems when installing the wedges. I figured the joints wouldn't split the sides as long as I tapped the wedges into their slots

until the tenon just filled the mortise. Of course, you don't want to drive the wedges with a 2-lb. club. I used a light hammer with a face just big enough to simultaneously strike both wedges into a tenon. I stopped tapping when I heard the pitch change as the wedges bottomed out solidly. When all the wedges were home, I cut off their protruding ends and then belt-sanded them flush with the sides.

With the case together, I measured for the chest's top, allowing it to overhang on three sides. When I cut out the top, I sawed the back edge square, but I sloped the overhanging sides by tilting my tablesaw blade to 70°. I hand-shaped the subtle edge curve on these three sides. After rabbeting the top for the back panel, I sanded both the top and the exterior of the sides. Next I drilled holes in the top and sides, and then I doweled and glued the top on.

Pulls, drawers, a back and a finish

It seems whenever two or more furniture-makers get together, the conversation always turns to handles and the restless hours a maker spends trying to integrate pulls into an overall design. I, too, have a healthy stash of failed handle mock-ups to kindle a fire during the winter. But I was pleased with the pulls I came up with for this chest of drawers (see the drawing detail on the facing page). The crossbar reflects the shape of the top of the chest, and the ends of the support pieces curve gently, like the front edges of the bureau's sides. One thing to remember: It's much easier to cut mortises or bore holes for the pulls before you glue up the drawers (the four drawers in my chest are dovetailed together the conventional way). This is also a good time to fit the drawer stops (I used ebony) in each divider.

After fitting the drawers, I screwed the chest's frame-and-panel back in place. Once I had the chest completely together, I applied four coats of Danish oil to the outside; the first coat diluted 50% with white spirits for better penetration, the second one straight from the can and the last two applied with a fine-grit (gray) Scotchbrite nylon pad.

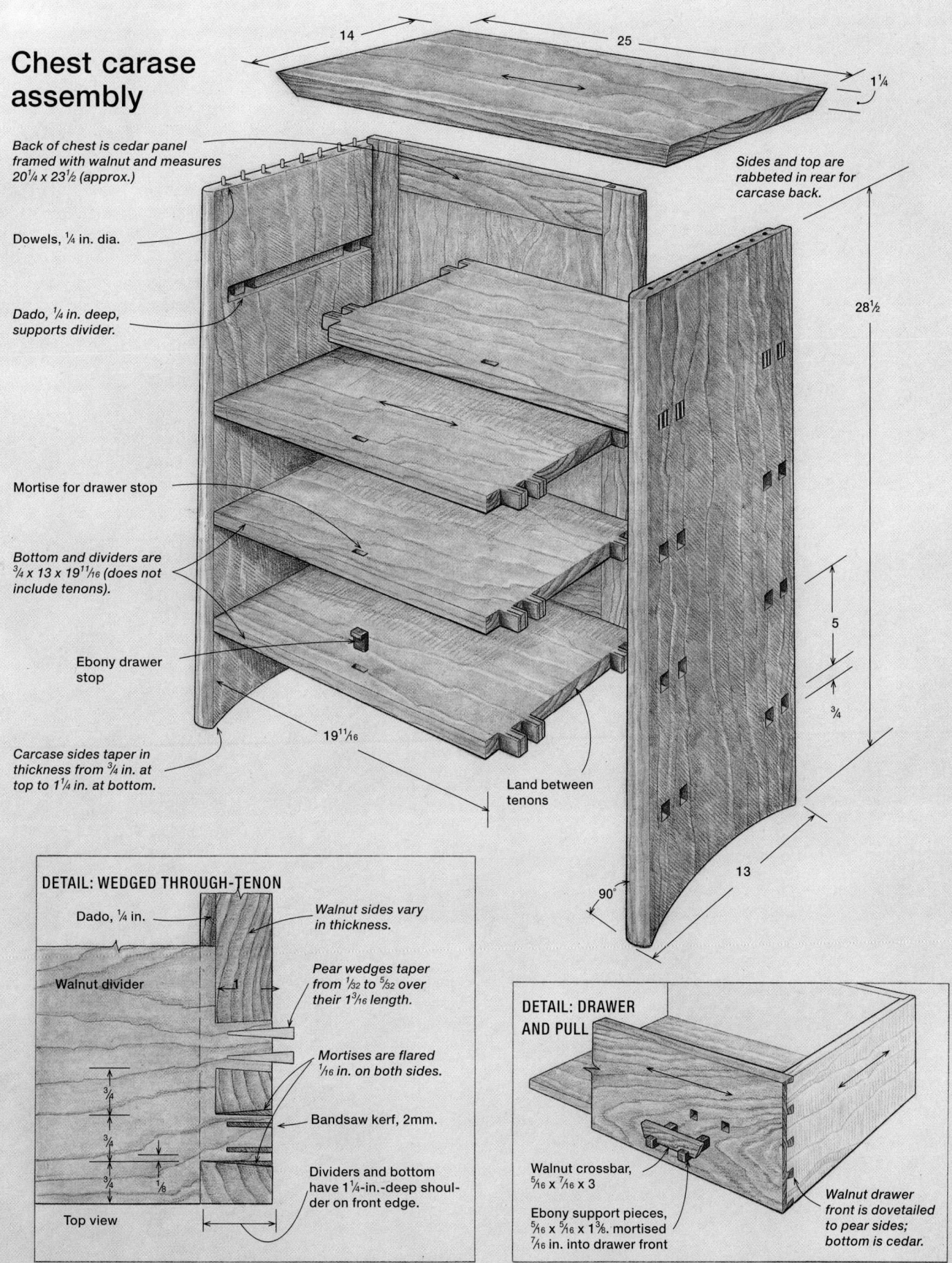

Chest carase assembly

14

25

1¼

Back of chest is cedar panel framed with walnut and measures 20¼ x 23½ (approx.)

Sides and top are rabbeted in rear for carcase back.

Dowels, ¼ in. dia.

Dado, ¼ in. deep, supports divider.

28½

Mortise for drawer stop

Bottom and dividers are ¾ x 13 x 19¹¹⁄₁₆ (does not include tenons).

Ebony drawer stop

5

¾

Carcase sides taper in thickness from ¾ in. at top to 1¼ in. at bottom.

19¹¹⁄₁₆

Land between tenons

90°

13

DETAIL: WEDGED THROUGH-TENON

Dado, ¼ in.

Walnut sides vary in thickness.

Walnut divider

1

Pear wedges taper from ¹⁄₃₂ to ⁵⁄₃₂ over their 1³⁄₁₆ length.

Mortises are flared ¹⁄₁₆ in. on both sides.

¾

¾

¾

⅛

Bandsaw kerf, 2mm.

Dividers and bottom have 1¼-in.-deep shoulder on front edge.

Top view

DETAIL: DRAWER AND PULL

Walnut crossbar, ⁵⁄₁₆ x ⁷⁄₁₆ x 3

Ebony support pieces, ⁵⁄₁₆ x ⁵⁄₁₆ x 1⅜ mortised ⁷⁄₁₆ in. into drawer front

Walnut drawer front is dovetailed to pear sides; bottom is cedar.

THREE

Drawers

Making drawers is like eating potato chips: one or two is rarely enough. Consider how many drawers need to be built for a single dresser. This has motivated woodworkers to find simple and fast ways to build them. And because the work is repetitive, production-style techniques and tools have evolved around drawer-making.

Dovetails are the joint of choice for drawers. They resist the types of stresses drawers undergo very, very well. For centuries dovetails were a job for handsaw, mallet, and chisel, but now they can be cut quickly and efficiently with a router and any one of a wide range of jigs designed specifically to cut the joint. If you have six drawers to make, that's 24 sets of dovetails. A router jig can cut your working time substantially, but most produce cookie-cutter dovetails instead of the unique dovetails that can be cut by hand.

Fitting drawers flush with a cabinet face is another job that always seems to take forever. Chris Becksvoort, however, applied the same logic Steve Latta did in the previous chapter and found a solution: the belt sander. Instead of trying to align each drawer front individually, Becksvoort sands the entire front face of the cabinet with drawers in place as if it were a tabletop that needed flattening. In a faction of the time traditional techniques take, all 15 drawers on his chest are trimmed flush.

On the other hand, you always have a choice of techniques depending on the end result you want. Speed and efficiency don't always have to be the primary goal. Drawers made to work perfectly rather than made in a rush before dinner add great value to a piece. Alan Peters shows you how. He has a way of fitting a drawer so well that a cushion of air softens movement in and out. This route ignores the production temptations of multiple drawers and intentionally requires that each drawer be fitted one by one. The results are drawers that are a pleasure to open and close.

JUST PLAIN DRAWERS

by John Lively

The built-ins and utility furniture I make usually call for lots of drawers. I could spend a couple of days hand-cutting the dovetails for a big case-work project. Or, going to the opposite extreme, I could rabbet and nail the drawers together and be done in a couple of hours. But what I really want is the strength and durability of dovetails, without spending the time it takes to do them by hand. That is why I cut the drawer joints for projects like the ones shown here with a router and dovetail fixture.

Router dovetails

I use an inexpensive router fixture I bought from Sears 20 years ago. It cuts only half-blind dovetails (meaning they're visible from one side only). Sears and most of the woodworking tool catalogs offer a similar fixture now for less than $100. I've thought about buying more expensive and more versatile fixtures that cut through dovetails, as well as half-blinds, and which promise the variable spacing of hand-cut work. But then I might as well cut them by hand if that's the look I'm after.

Hand-cut dovetails consist of pins, which are typically cut on drawer fronts and backs, and tails, which are cut on drawer sides, as shown on the facing page. Router dovetails, however, get pins on the drawer sides and sockets on the fronts and backs. With hand-cut dovetails, you can tailor the joint to suit the dimensions of the piece. With router dovetails, you can't.

Router dovetails are ideal for built-in drawers like these in a floor-to-ceiling storage center. Sturdy, durable dovetail joints you can cut without any fuss are a great improvement over the nailed rabbet joints usually found in these situations.

One thing that makes router dovetails fast is that you don't have to lay them out. The fixture clamps two boards at 90° to each other (drawer front or back on top, side hanging down). On top of both boards goes a finger template that controls the router and dovetail bit by means of a template-following guide bushing. The thickness of the drawer stock can vary from a little less than $\frac{1}{2}$ inch to more than one inch. Width can vary too, from about three inches to 12 inches. But regardless of the width and thickness, the size and geometry of the pins and sockets stay the same.

That means you have to size your drawers to the geometry of this cookie-cutter joint. You want to end up either with a whole pin at the top of the joint or a half-pin. Anything less than a half-pin looks awkward and is liable to splinter away.

Two adjustments control the fit of the joint. The router's vertical depth of cut determines whether the joint is too loose, too tight or just right. The in/out positioning of the finger template controls the lateral travel of the router and thereby determines the depth of the sockets. If the sockets are too deep, the drawer sides will be recessed below the ends of the front and back; if the sockets are too shallow, the drawer sides will stand proud.

Workmanlike utility furnishings, like the author's little cabinet for storing nails and screws, make the shop efficient and pleasant. Rabbeted corners, screwed and plugged, join the pine case, which measures 17 in. by 24 in. by 10½ in. deep.

Once the fixture and router are set up and adjusted, you can cut both parts of the joint at once. When you get used to the routine, clamping up the stock, routing and unclamping take only a couple of minutes. Doing the joints for an entire drawer takes less than ten minutes.

This method lets me complete and fit six drawers, pretty much regardless of size, in about as many hours, starting from uncut (but thicknessed) stock. What about the time it takes to set up the router and fine-tune the cut? You can eliminate that completely, as explained in the sidebar on p. 58.

Hand-cut vs. router-cut dovetails

The beauty of hand-cut dovetails comes from proportions that suit the project. Router dovetails have equally sized pins and sockets, so the project must be dimensioned to avoid awkward part-pins.

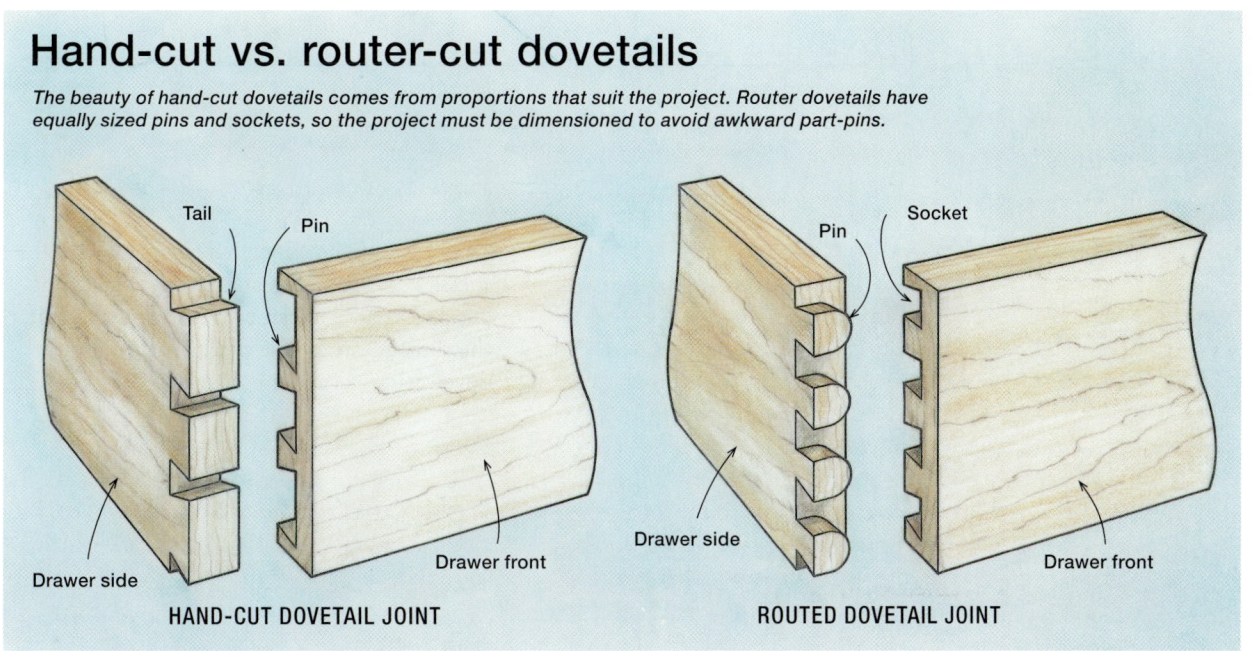

Tail   Pin

Drawer side   Drawer front

HAND-CUT DOVETAIL JOINT

Pin   Socket

Drawer side   Drawer front

ROUTED DOVETAIL JOINT

Ditzy setup: what the manual won't tell you

The owner's manual for your dovetail fixture will cover the details of setting up, but there are some important points that it probably won't mention.

The precise depth of cut, which determines joint tightness, seldom is exactly what the manual calls for. My Sears manual says to set the cutting depth to exactly 1$\frac{1}{32}$ in., a measurement that requires a machinist's combination square and a thick magnifying lens for people over 40. But setting my carbide dovetail bit by this rule produces too loose a joint. A slightly deeper cut tightens the joint. The owner's manual will get you in the ballpark, but you'll have to discover the setting that's right for your bit, router and template (see the photo at right).

Another thing the owner's manual won't explain is what's too tight a joint and what's too loose. What I've learned is that glue takes up space, and a joint that I have to tap together dry, I'll have to bang together during glue-up. You should be able to push the dry joint together by hand without recourse to your mallet.

The manual describes how to control socket depth, but it probably won't discuss the correct depth. If you've cut your drawer fronts to fit snugly in their openings, then you want the pins on the drawer sides to lie about $\frac{1}{64}$ in. below the tops of their sockets. This condition lets you beltsand the endgrain edges of the front and back flush with the sides and provides just enough clearance between the sides of the drawer and the opening. If you do this right, the side-to-side fit should require no further fiddling.

No manual will admit that setting up and adjusting both router and fixture is tedious and time-wasting. It can take a half-hour to go through the steps: install the guide bushing in your router, chuck and adjust the bit, make a trial cut, fine-tune the depth of cut, try again. At last you've got it. But next time, you'll have to go through the whole ditzy routine again.

About six years ago, I got fed up with setting up, so I went out and bought myself a new plunge router. This meant I could dedicate my old Sears router to dovetails, and since then, I haven't had to remove the bushing or adjust the bit.

Bit setting determines joint tightness. Owner's manuals typically specify a depth-of-cut setting, which determines how the joint fits. The deeper the cut, the tighter the joint. But finding that just-right setting for your router and template is really a matter of tedious trial and error. A carbide-tipped bit is best for dovetailing because you cut to full depth in a single pass, which calls for cutting edges that stay sharp.

Buy unwarped stock

For the drawer sides and backs of utility projects, I buy 8-ft. planks of 1x12 #2 pine from the local lumberyard. Lauan and poplar are also good choices, although better suited to more upscale projects. Find a yard that will let you pick through the stock. Prepare to spend some time eyeballing the planks. Everybody wants to buy boards as knot-free as #2 grading will allow. But in selecting drawer stock, wood clarity is less desirable than flatness. You want pieces free of twist and cup, though a slight bow or crook is tolerable. Reject those twisted and cupped boards because you'll pay the devil later if you don't. Twisted boards make twisted drawers that will never fit right, and cupped stock requires a lot of fussy clamping during glue-up.

So what I do first is select the flat stuff and then go through it for clarity. I avoid boards with a lot of large knots or with any loose knots. And when I plan to make the fronts out of pine, I make sure the boards have enough clear cuttings in them.

Carefully arrange the parts of each drawer to keep track of the pieces. Stand them up drawer-wise behind the dovetail jig, then push them over flat so their bottom, inside edges, marked with pencil for grooving, face one another.

Steer the router in and out of the template slots by pressing its guide bushing against the phenolic plastic. Make a light climb cut from right to left, then return left to right at full depth. The router always exits horizontally (an upward exit would chew into the template).

Position the parts in the jig. Clamp up the front right corner of the drawer. Insides of the pieces face out, the drawer front goes on top, and the side goes vertical. Both pieces index hard against the jig's registration pins, one of which is visible by the author's right thumb. The black plastic comb is the template that guides the router.

Rip first, then crosscut

Pine 1x12s are about 11 inches wide and three-fourths inch thick, and unless your drawers are really deep and wide, you can get several drawers out of a single board. Start by jointing one edge of the 8-footer, and then rip to width, larger drawers first. Avoid the temptation to rip slightly undersized to eliminate trimming to fit later. Every time I have done this, I've been sorry. Shoot for parts that fit snugly in their openings.

Another reason for ripping first is that long offcuts are good for moldings, battens, cleats, face frames, story poles and tomato stakes. Long scrap is always more useful than short scrap.

While drawers for a single project may vary in depth, most likely they will all be uniform in plan. This means you can set a saw stop and crosscut all the fronts and backs in one session, all the sides in another. Use a clean-cutting crosscut blade here because rough endgrain won't glue well and because ragged edges will show up in the joints and on the faces of the pins. One more thing: you don't want knots in the joints, so be sure to crosscut so all knots are two inches or more away from the ends.

Now stack the drawer parts in discrete piles. From this point on, each drawer is a family of four members, and shuffling them around will introduce error.

Which piece goes where

Begin by clamping the fixture to your bench. Take a stack of drawer parts and mark their outside faces. Draw lines about where you'll plow the grooves for the drawer bottom. On the bench immediately behind

The completed joint, still in the jig, shows how pins (on vertical board) will interlock with sockets (on horizontal board). Routing four joints takes less than ten minutes.

Use a stiff brush to work glue down into the pins. Don't apply glue in the sockets because it can pool up and keep the joint from closing.

the fixture, stand the members on their bottom edges and position them just as they'll be in the finished drawer, with the front facing you. Now push the sides over flat, as shown in the top left photo on p. 59. The lines representing the grooves will keep you oriented when you clamp the pieces into the fixture. You'll need the help because they go into the fixture inside out and backward, and it's easy to get confused.

I begin at the front right-hand corner of the drawer, which means that I clamp it on the right side of the fixture with its bottom edges facing right. Temporarily clamp up the drawer side, so its end protrudes about half its thickness above the baseplate of the fixture. Now slide the drawer front under the clamp bar, and butt its end against the protruding drawer side. At the same time,

shove the front into contact with the fixture's registration pin.

When the joint end of the drawer front butts hard against the side and its bottom edge hard against the registration pin, tighten the clamp bar. A little pressure here goes a long way. Now put the finger template in position, and tighten its locking knobs. Next, back off on the vertical clamp bar, and raise the drawer side up flush against the finger template. To keep the template from flexing upward, hold it down firmly with one hand while you butt the drawer side into it with the other. Once the board is in position, hold it there with your thumb, and tighten the clamp bar, as shown in the bottom photo on p. 59.

Give everything a final check to make sure you've properly positioned the pieces. The drawer front should be on top, the drawer side should hang down vertically. The inside faces of the front and side should face out with the groove lines to the outside. Both pieces must be indexed tight against the registration pins. Be sure about this because imprecise registration will make a joint that doesn't fit. If you mix up the pieces, you'll cut the pins on the wrong board, which means wasting wood and wasting time.

Driving the router

The actual routing is surprisingly quick. Hold the router firmly down against the finger template while cutting, and never lift it upward. If you do, the bit will cut through wood you don't want to waste, and possibly through the template as well. Always exit the cut by pulling the router out horizontally.

Begin routing by making a light right-to-left pass down the front of the drawer side. If you take too deep a bite when cutting right to left (climb cutting), the router will self-feed right into the fixture, so go easy. This initial cut keeps the bit from tearing out the wood at the base of the joint.

Now you're at the left side of the joint. Follow the finger template in and out, moving the router from left to right. As you round the template fingers, twist the router slightly counterclockwise, as shown in the top right photo on p. 59. This helps you negotiate these hairpin curves smoothly and

quickly. Because you're cutting to full depth in a single pass, don't force the router. Listen to the bit's whine, and if its bright voice begins to dull, slow down. But don't go so slowly that you burn the stock and glaze or overheat the bit. A carbide-tipped dovetail bit will put less stress on you and your router.

After cutting the joints for the front right corner, go to the front left, then to the left rear and, finally, to the right rear, moving around the drawer in a clockwise manner. The drawer front or back always goes horizontal on top of the fixture; the side always goes vertical. Before moving on to the next drawer, mark conjoining parts with a number, so the joints that were cut together will be assembled together.

Grooves for drawer bottoms

For drawer bottoms, I use 5mm lauan plywood captured in grooves on all four sides. Rather than use a dado set to cut a $\frac{1}{4}$-in. groove, too wide for standard plywood, I make two passes on the tablesaw to make a groove that leaves but a little play.

Set the rip fence so that the first pass cuts just to the inside of the bottom socket on the drawer back and the blade depth to cut clear of the bottom of the socket. Now saw the first groove on all the drawer members, making sure to register the bottom edge of each against the fence. Your pencil line helps here. Move the fence and make the second series of cuts. One nice thing about router dovetails is that you don't have to stop any grooves in the drawer fronts or backs because the groove enters in and exits from a socket, which gets filled with a pin.

Dry-assemble one drawer to measure the length and width of the drawer bottoms. Cut the plywood about $\frac{1}{16}$ inch shy of the full dimension to ensure that your joints will close completely on the first try.

Assembly and glue-up

The fastest way to get good glue coverage is to paint the pins with a stiff bristle brush. While you're clamping up one drawer, keep the brush soaking in a jar of water, and wipe it dry when you're ready to glue up the next one. Squirt a couple of tablespoons of yellow glue into a shallow container—I use a plastic coffee-can lid—so you can dip your

brush often. Thoroughly coat the pins on both ends of one drawer side (see the bottom photo on the facing page). Now slip the drawer front and back onto the pins, and lightly tap the joint together. Slide the bottom into the grooves, apply glue to the pins on the other drawer side and tap it into the sockets.

Squeeze the whole thing together with bar clamps and blocks. Position the blocks at the baseline of the pins, so the clamping pressure will pull the sides until the pins bottom out in their sockets, as shown in the photo above.

Fitting the drawers

If you've cut the drawer members to fit tightly, the assembled drawer won't slide freely in its opening and might not even enter. To trim it for an easy fit, beltsand the endgrain edges of the front and back flush with the sides. Test fit the drawer. If it still won't go into the opening, most likely the sides are a bit too wide, so handplane a little off the top and bottom edges all around until the drawer runs in and out without binding. Chamfer all the inside and outside edges (block plane or router), and wax the edges top and bottom, along with the back outside corners.

There's a sweet place in fitting a drawer. If you don't trim it down enough, it will fit too tightly and bind. The same thing will happen if you remove too much wood because the drawer will cock in its opening and bind. And, to make a bad matter worse, too much air around a drawer's edges looks sloppy. But if you trim off just the right amount, the drawer will whisper in and out.

FITTING
A DRAWER

by Alan Peters

My wife, Laura, doesn't understand why I make such a fuss about drawer fitting. The drawers in our kitchen cabinets slide on plastic runners, and she says they work better than the drawers in any of my furniture. I can't argue with that—those nylon rollers do their job well. But plastic slides don't belong on dovetailed drawers. Fine furniture requires another solution, an approach that substitutes craftsmanship for the manufactured precision of drawer slides.

The technique we use in my workshop involves three successive levels of fitting. The first is of the individual drawer parts, then the assembled drawer without its bottom and, finally, the drawer with its bottom installed. The result is a drawer that fits so well that it's slowed by a cushion of air as you push it in. And when you pull out the drawer, any other drawers in the case are gently pulled back into the nearly airtight case. It takes time to achieve this piston fit, but the results speak for themselves. Other furnituremakers may pride themselves on their dovetails or some other joinery, but for me, a finely fitted drawer is the benchmark of a craftsman's skill.

Well-built drawers start with stable wood

Drawer sides should only be made of top-quality, mild-grained and, preferably, quartersawn stock. What you are looking for is wood that will remain straight, move very little with shifts in humidity and plane easily and cleanly. At the top of my list is Honduras mahogany. Most of my drawer sides are made of material salvaged from old, factory-made mahogany furniture. Because of its age, the wood is about as stable as it's ever going to be. After

mahogany, quartersawn oak is my choice for drawer sides.

I make my choice depending on the wood used for the drawer fronts, always aiming for a contrast in color. I like mahogany with lighter colored drawer fronts, such as ash or sycamore, and oak sides when the drawer fronts are made of darker woods, such as walnut or rosewood. From time to time, I use other woods, such as teak, because it wears so well, and rippled (curly) sycamore on special cabinets or desks, where the visual quality of the drawer sides is very important.

Fit the drawer pieces individually and precisely

Regardless of how much care you put into making and fitting the drawer, it will not fit well if the opening in the case is not consistent front to back and top to bottom. Check the openings, and true them with a shoulder plane if necessary. Make sure, above all, that the case doesn't taper in from front to back. Once the case is trued up, sand the inside, and polish it with a good-quality paste wax.

I don't make or fit drawers on damp or particularly humid days. Instead, I'll wait for a dry spell so that the drawer parts aren't swollen with moisture. Also, whenever possible, I bring the drawer stock into the shop to acclimate for a few weeks before dimensioning it.

Fit the sides first, top to bottom

The first step in fitting the drawer pieces is to cut them to rough size, say, within $\frac{1}{8}$ in. of finished length and width. All pieces can be thicknessed to final dimension, as long as you bear in mind that you'll be planing and sanding them slightly to fit. Before I do any

Fitting drawer parts

1. Mark the drawer sides. Because each drawer is fit precisely to a particular opening, the location and orientation of each part is marked.

2. Shoot the edge. A sharp jointer plane and a shooting board will give you a straight edge that's 90° to the face of the drawer side. A little wax on the sole and side of the plane will help it glide better.

3. Snug but not binding—When the sides will just slide in and out without binding in the case, they're fit. If they do bind, look for shiny spots on the top edge, which indicate high spots.

The sides have been fitted. The drawer backs are next. Colored dots at the corners of the case piece identify mating edges and indicate the front of the case.

planing, I use a pair of winding sticks to be sure that all pieces are flat.

I work with the sides first, testing both faces of each side to see which planes better. I choose this side for the face because it will have to be planed to fit and mark it accordingly (see the top left photo on p. 63). If there's more than one drawer, I also indicate which drawer the part belongs to. The end of the drawer where I start my plane stroke becomes the front end so that all fitting is from front to back. If one edge of a drawer side is more difficult to plane, I try to make it the bottom edge because the top edge is where all the planing to fit takes place. Then I plane the inside of the drawer and sand it with 400-grit paper. After this, I shouldn't have to do anything more other than apply a coat of paste wax.

I cut the sides to length on the tablesaw and then plane the bottom edges on a shooting board. I saw the other edges to within $1/16$ in. of the finished width (or less) and then plane them, too, on the shooting board (see the top right photo on p. 63). After nearly every pass with the plane, I check the fit in the case. If it binds, I check the top edge to see where it's burnished,

Drawer backs are next

Fit the backs from side to side. Check the fit often because only one stroke of the plane separates a drawer that fits from one that's sloppy. These drawer backs have been cut to width to fit over drawer bottoms.

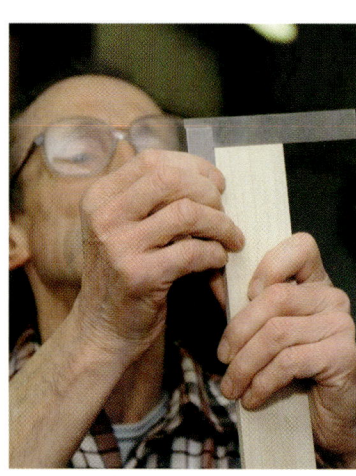

indicating rubbing between the drawer side and the case, and remove a shaving there. When the side goes all the way home without binding, but still requires a fair amount of force, it's ready (see the bottom photo on p. 63). There should be no play at all. Further fitting, which will make the drawer side move more freely, will take place after the drawer has been assembled. Repeat the process for all drawer sides in the case.

Fit the back perfectly

A perfect fit for the back is absolutely essential because it is used as the pattern for the front. With large drawers, I fit each back precisely to its opening, so it just snugs into the case opening on all four sides. This is important, because the opening often will not be perfectly square. Fitting the back (and then front) of the drawer to the opening helps to ensure a perfect fit.

On small drawers, however, like the ones in this desktop unit, it's less important to fit the drawer backs from top to bottom. Because the drawers are so narrow, only the lengths of the backs need to be fit to the case openings. Openings this small can't be out of square by very much.

Drawer fronts are last

1

Mark the fronts from the backs. Because the backs fit snugly from end to end (and on large drawers, from top to bottom), they can be used to lay out the fronts. Marking with a knife gives the author a precise line that he extends across the face of the drawer front with a small square.

2

Plane a slight bevel on the ends. This inward taper helps with the fitting of the drawer front.

3

Fitting the fronts—With the fronts snugged into place, no light or gaps should be visible at the top, bottom or sides.

Fronts are fitted. With all drawer parts fit to their openings, the drawers can now be dovetailed together.

after each stroke (see the bottom right photo on p. 64).

To prevent end-grain tearout at the edge of the board (what we call spelching here in England), I pivot the plane nearly 90° to the direction of cut as I complete the stroke. This way, the blade cuts across the fibers at the edge of the board rather than catching them and breaking them off. There should be no gap at all at the ends of the backs when they're in place in the case.

The front should fit like a plug

I mark out the length of the front by placing the corresponding back on it, with the bottom edges flush, and knifing marks at either end of the back (see the top photo on p. 65). After shooting the bottom edge of the front, I saw and then plane the top edge to fit, beveling it ever so slightly front to back. I check the fit after each stroke, holding the piece in its opening at an angle (because it hasn't been cut to length yet), being extremely careful not to take off too much with any one pass.

I fit the front from end to end in the same way that I do the back, except that I bevel the ends slightly, just like the top (see the left photo on p. 65). The front should fit its opening exactly, with no gaps around it at all (see the bottom right photo on p. 65).

Fitting the drawer box

Drawer joinery is another subject entirely—far too big to include here. Suffice it to say that any drawer worth fitting this well has been properly dovetailed. And be sure to mark out the dovetails so the tails stand slightly proud of the pins. The front and back of each drawer have been fitted precisely to the opening, so you'll want to remove material from the drawer sides, not from the ends of the front or back, which are your reference lengths.

When I glue up a dovetailed drawer, I don't use any clamps, relying instead on the accuracy of the joints to hold the drawer together. I use glue very sparingly and just tap the dovetails home with a hammer. I use a block of wood to prevent the surface of the drawer sides from being marred. The same goes for mortises and tenons, which I sometimes use to attach the back to the sides as I did on this drawer. Extending the

I mark the backs by indicating which drawer each one belongs to and writing this number on a little round paper dot that I can peel off later (see the bottom right photo on p. 64). I stick the dot on the inside of the drawer—facing the front of the cabinet, at the top—so I know how the back is supposed to be oriented throughout the fitting process.

To prepare the back, I shoot the bottom edge and then saw and plane the top edge to width to fit snugly in the drawer opening. Then I'll transfer the outline of the drawer back to the front before cutting the back to width to fit over the drawer bottom, which slides beneath it. In the case of a small drawer, though, I just cut and plane the back to width right away. I get this measurement—from the top of the drawer bottom groove to the top of the opening—from my full-scale drawing.

Next I shoot one end of the back square, set it in place in the opening and then position the other end as closely as possible to where it belongs. I make a pencil mark at this end, cut the back just a hair long and then plane it to fit, checking it in the case sides past the back allows the drawer to open fully without dropping out of its opening. Whatever the construction, if a drawer is going to fit its opening well, it's important to compare measurements from corner to corner when gluing up and to make adjustments to get the drawer square (see the photo below).

A drawer board supports the drawer as you plane

Once the glue has cured (I wait several hours at least, but overnight is better), I take a chisel and pare away the top back corner of both sides (see the top left photo on p. 68). If the back corner was dovetailed, often it will have swollen up because of the moisture introduced by the glue. Even if that's not the case, taking down this corner will prevent the drawer from binding as it enters the case. I also ease all the arrises (the sharp corners where edge meets side) with a

block plane followed by some fine sandpaper, and I soften the top edge of the drawer back.

I leave the bottom out at this stage so I can position the drawer over a drawer board to plane the sides (see the top right photo on p. 68). The drawer board fully supports the drawer but doesn't get in the way of the plane. The drawer board should fit quite accurately between the inside faces of the drawer front and back.

I take a few passes with a plane to bring the sides flush with the end grain of the drawer front and back and then check the fit of the drawer in its opening. I leave just a little sanding or planing to do after the drawer bottom is installed. I slide the drawer in and out of its opening rapidly a few times. This burnishes the sides and top edges of the drawer sides wherever they're rubbing against the case. I plane away these burnished (shiny) spots and check the fit again.

Fitting drawers to the case

MAKE IT SQUARE

Make sure the drawer glues up square. As soon as the joints are together, compare diagonals and adjust the drawer box if necessary.

Trim to fit

1. Pare away the top back corner. This will prevent the drawer from binding as you try to fit it into its opening.

2. Clean up the sides. A few strokes with a plane will bring the sides flush with the end grain of the front and back, which have been fit precisely and should not be planed further.

3. Plane stops to position drawer front. If you have more than one drawer stop per drawer, remove material evenly from each.

Section through drawer stop

Plane front of stop

Rail

Wood grain for stop is oriented vertically for strength.

This process is repeated until the drawer will move in and out with relative ease, but no slop. The closer I get to a fit, the more often I check.

As you're planing the drawer sides, be careful not to remove too much material from the edge of the drawer front, where it would be visible from the front of the case. After cleaning up the dovetails, I often won't touch this area with a plane again. I just sand it lightly until the fit is right.

Final fit is with the drawer bottom in place

Once the drawer is sliding nicely in its opening, it's time to put the drawer bottom in. I almost always use solid cedar of Lebanon. It smells nice, my clients like it and it keeps moths and worms away. Because it's solid wood, I orient the grain from side to side so that any expansion is front to back. I spot-glue the bottom at the front so that no gap opens up there, and I screw the bottom to the back using slotted screw holes so the bottom can move.

To make sure that the bottom is seated in its groove all the way along its length, I set the drawer on the bench on one side and then tap on the other with a hammer. A piece of scrap protects the side that's being hammered. I repeat the process on the other side.

Next I check the fit of the drawer in its opening. Often it will need no further fitting. If it's a little snug, removing a shaving or two is the most that will be necessary. A light sanding with 400-grit usually will do.

With the drawer fit, I make sure all outer faces and edges are sanded to 400-grit (the insides have already been done). Then I apply a coat of paste wax to all surfaces except the face of the drawer front. It will be finished with the case later.

Drawer stop determines the position of the front

All that remains is to get the plane of the drawer front where you want it—either flush with the sides of the case or back a bit if you prefer. Many furnituremakers simply glue a small block of wood to the drawer divider for a drawer stop, perhaps affixing a piece of leather or felt to cushion the impact. Unfortunately, this type of drawer stop will almost always get knocked out over time.

In my shop, we prevent this problem by mortising L-shaped drawer stops into the drawer dividers (mortises are cut before the case is assembled). The grain of the drawer stop is oriented vertically, perpendicular to the dividers. No amount of force will break off a stop like this, and the leg of the L-shape gives me material to plane away to get the drawer to stop where I want it (see the bottom photo and drawing on the facing page).

I check the drawer in its opening once more, this time to see how much material I must remove from the front of the stop. A few passes with a bullnose plane and the job is done. If you have more than one stop (I usually use two, one near either case side), try to remove material evenly from both stops. To see if you've succeeded, place a little pressure against the drawer front right in front of one of the stops. If the drawer front gives at all, the stop behind it has had more material removed from it. The other one will need a shaving or two removed to even things up. As always, the closer I get to where I want to be, the more cautiously I proceed.

The result is a drawer that fits so well it's slowed by a cushion of air as you push it in. And when you pull out the drawer, any other drawers in the case are gently pulled back into the nearly airtight case.

DRAWER FRONTS THAT FIT FLUSH

by Christian H. Becksvoort

Maintaining drawer-front alignment to the face frame can be a seasonal problem on furniture built with slab (or wide board) construction and typical rear-mounted drawer stops. The depth of the case can vary considerably from summer to winter depending upon the width, species and cut of the wood. The length of wood does not change noticeably with changes in moisture content, however, so flush-mounted drawers with stops at the back tend to protrude in the winter and are recessed in the summer.

I've borrowed a technique of front-mounted drawer stops from an antique piece and have used it quite successfully for the last several years. Front-stopped drawers always maintain the same position in relation to the front of the cabinet, and they don't need to be individually adjusted for each drawer. This technique uses a stop glued to the divider under the drawer instead of placing the stop at the back of the drawer.

The stops also help me sand the drawer fronts and cabinet front at the same time, ensuring a flat, smooth plane and perfect drawer alignment. I install the drawers in the carcase against the stops and wedge them in place. I then beltsand the entire front of the case, including drawer fronts, drawer dividers and the front edges of the cabinet sides, as shown in the photo on

Aligning the front on a chest of drawers— The author has developed a technique for beltsanding his cabinet fronts and drawers at the same time. When he combines them with front-mounted stops, the cabinet faces are flat and smooth and drawers always align with the face frame, regardless of season.

Scribed lines accurately position stops—The author uses a 4-in.- to 6-in.-wide board, cut to the appropriate length, as a gauge to scribe alignment marks for the drawer stops. Measuring from the cabinet back eliminates any variations that may have occurred when gluing in the dovetailed drawer dividers.

p. 73. The drawers support the belt sander, so I don't have to worry about balancing it on the thin dividers and gouging the case sides when I sand to the edge of the case. While sanding the drawer fronts, I'm also able to sand out all the minor misalignment that occurs when sliding the dovetailed dividers into place in the case sides.

There is no other technique that will leave the case and drawers as flat and as perfectly aligned. The whole system works because I house my drawer bottoms in grooves that are $5/16$ in. from the bottom edge of the drawers. This leaves plenty of clearance for the $1/4$-in.-thick drawer stops glued to the drawer divider below the drawer. The stops are out of sight and don't interfere with the drawer's contents as top-mounted stops might.

The drawer stops are glued, positioned on the dividers and held in place with spring clamps. The stops must be thin enough to clear the drawer bottoms and short enough to allow drawer side clearance at the ends. Leather bumpers are temporarily glued to the stops to position the drawers for sanding.

Fitting the stops

First I fit the drawers, leaving about $1/32$-in. to $3/64$-in. gap on either side, and a gap above the drawer appropriate to the size, species and moisture content of the drawer front. I also make the drawers short enough (about $1/2$-in. shy of the full cabinet depth) to accommodate more than the full range of movement expected in the cabinet side.

Wedging the drawers in place holds them for beltsanding. The drawers should be wedged on each side to center them in the opening and wedged at the top to hold them firmly against the drawer dividers and stops. The entire front of the cabinet can then be sanded to one flat, smooth plane.

Then I mark the location of the stops, referencing from the back of the case. If this were a perfect world, I could simply mark from the front of the case, allowing for the thickness of the drawer front and the leather bumper. But perfectly aligning the snug, sliding dovetail joints that connect the dividers to the carcase is not an easy task. Sometimes the glue grabs before the divider is fully seated; other times that last tap knocks the divider $1/16$ in. past where you want it, and no amount of pounding will reverse it. Referencing the stops from the back of the case lets me sand out misalignments when I'm sanding the drawer fronts to align with the case.

To make sure that all the stops are aligned, first I find the divider that is inset the farthest. I measure from the front of this divider, deducting the thickness of the drawer front plus a leather bumper. This mark is where the front of the stop needs to be to leave the drawer front flush with the divider's face. I then make a gauge for marking the rest of the dividers by measuring from the back of the cabinet to the mark. I cut a 4-in.- to 6-in.-wide scrap board to that length to serve as a guide for laying out all the stops. The gauge is slipped into the opening, making sure it is pushed tightly against the cabinet back and side, so all the drawers will be equidistant from the back of

the cabinet. The stop position is marked by scribing a line along the front edge of the measuring gauge, as shown in the top photo. I find that a knife-scribed line is more accurate than a pencil line when marking the stops. To make the scribed line more visible, you can darken it by running a pencil sharpened to a chisel point along the line.

I cut the stops from waste stock, $3/8$ in. to $1/2$ in. wide and $1/4$ in. thick. For drawers 14 in. and narrower, I usually use a single strip across the divider. The strips are centered in the drawer opening, and they leave plenty of room on each side for the $1/2$-in.-thick drawer sides. Wider drawers get two stops about 2 in. to 3 in. long. After sanding, the stops are glued to the scribed lines and held in place with spring clamps (see the bottom photo on p. 71). The stops must be located about 1 in. from the carcase sides so they don't interfere with the drawer sides. Then the leather bumpers are temporarily glued to the fronts of the stops, using a minute amount of glue. After the front has been sanded, the leather is removed for finishing (otherwise it becomes hard) and reapplied when the case is complete. I prefer the quality feel and sound of leather bumpers on a custom piece because they make a better impression than the rubber, plastic or cork bumpers so frequently found on store-bought furniture.

Sanding the cabinet front, with the drawers held in place by front-mounted stops and wedges, ensures that the entire face of the cabinet will be flat and smooth. The drawers support the sander and prevent gouging the face frame. This technique eliminates the need to set each drawer individually.

Sanding the case and drawers

The first time I used this method of stopping drawers, it dawned on me that this was the perfect solution to sanding the entire cabinet face. No more balancing a belt sander on a $^3/_4$-in.-wide divider, hoping not to gouge the cabinet side or intersecting dividers. This was a real bonus. It takes a little preparation, but the results are well worth the effort.

First, after drilling holes for hardware or knobs in the drawer fronts, I slide all the drawers back into the case. Next I make shims, using $^1/_{16}$-in. by $^1/_2$-in. pine strips, tapering the ends into wedges with a quick knife cut. I shim the drawer sides to center the drawer from side to side in the opening, as shown in the photo on the facing page. Then, using thicker pine strips, I shim the top of the drawer front to hold the drawer against the divider below it. The shims should be good and tight to keep the drawer from vibrating during the sanding process.

With all the drawers securely in place, I lay the cabinet on its back on two padded sawhorses of convenient height. Using a belt sander and an 80-grit belt, I work my way across the face of the cabinet, from one end to the other, as shown in the bottom photo on this page. Before sanding with a 120-grit belt, I check the cabinet face for high and low spots by laying a 5-ft.-long straightedge on the face of the cabinet and sighting along the straightedge's bottom edge. I repeat the process in four or five places across the cabinet face, marking the high spots with a pencil line. I then connect these marks, making a topographical map, of sorts, on the cabinet face to show me where more material needs to be removed. After sanding with 120-grit and 150-grit belts, I switch to a vibrating-pad sander or random-orbit sander and 180-grit, 220-grit and 320-grit discs.

Finishing details

At this point, the front of the cabinet is a single, flat, smooth plane. I remove the drawers for a final hand-sanding with a bolt through the knob hole. The first drawer is always difficult to remove, especially if the shimming was done correctly and you forgot to drill the knob holes before wedging in the drawers. However, once the first one is out, I have room to reach in and push out the rest from behind. I hand-sand each drawer face with 400-grit paper and ease and smooth all the edges. The same goes for the cabinet face: Remove all traces of cross-grain scratches and break all edges. Then vacuum out the inside of the case, remove the leather bumpers and the case is ready for the finish of your choice.

FOUR

Doors

As a rule, "make it simple" is easy to remember but very hard to master. It is perhaps the most important technique a woodworker can apply to his work. We learn by doing, and so tend to figure something out as we're doing it. This often leads to roundabout solutions, which we stick with because they work. And once learned, they are hard to unlearn.

When confronted with a new, simpler way of doing something, the reaction is often to look for the problems. If none are easily found, it's time to look harder for the problem until one is found, rather than accept the new technique. Many woodworkers, if not most, still persist in techniques that are a bit slower, a bit less efficient, and less troublesome simply because they like them. And when it comes down to it, there isn't anything terribly wrong in that.

For example, door construction is one of the more contentious issues among woodworkers. Because doors are free-floating and unsupported by another part of the cabinet or house, they need to be strong. Doors undergo a much greater range of stresses than most furniture (with the exception of chairs). Badly built doors, especially exterior doors, don't last long, sagging away from the hinges and scraping the jamb and floor. The traditional door joint is the mortise and tenon, which is very strong and has a great track record for standing up to long-term use and abuse. There are door builders who will swear that anything less than a mortise and tenon is not enough.

In this section, you'll find techniques for a traditional small cabinet door, made efficiently with mortise-and-tenon joints, and a full-sized interior door made with non-traditional biscuits. Is the world turned on its head? Of course not. Simplicity has simply intruded on tradition and come up with a new technique. Is it better? That depends entirely on what your goals are, and what you prefer. Mortise-and-tenon joints are not particularly efficient, while biscuits are. Mortise-and-tenon joints are probably stronger, but do small interior doors need it? Listen to a woodworker who "made it simple" before you decide.

QUICK BUT STURDY CABINET DOOR

by Mario Rodriguez

Quirk-and-bead molding and an antiqued stain and lacquer finish give the author's pine, plywood-paneled door an air of simple period elegance.

When I had to make a batch of pantry cabinets in a hurry and at a low cost, I developed the design for this frame-and-panel door. I wanted the door to have a traditional flavor and reasonable strength but obtained with the least possible labor and materials. I decided to use a plywood panel and dress it up with a simple quirk-and-bead molding, as shown in the photo at left. I planned the simplest joinery I could, and then I decided to apply the molding instead of milling it onto the frame pieces. The molding is easily made with a stock router bit, and the quirk, or recess, behind the bead produces a dramatic shadow that gives the flat-paneled door its visual weight. The design is well-suited for small- or medium-sized doors on kitchen cabinets, vanities and built-in storage units and will look as good painted as with a clear finish.

Grooving non-stop

I chose $\frac{1}{4}$-in. plywood (good on both sides) for the panel to keep the door light and stock preparation to a minimum. Frame-and-panel construction accommodates the expansion and contraction of a solid panel by allowing it to float in the frame. Here, with no wood movement to worry about, I was able to glue the panel on all four sides, making it a structural element of the door. I greatly simplified the joinery by housing both the panel and the rail tenons in the same $\frac{3}{4}$-in.-deep groove (see the drawing on the facing page). At $\frac{3}{4}$ in., the tenons are somewhat short, but the plywood panel glued all the way around at full depth in the groove adds considerably to the door's strength.

This technique not only removes the need for making separate mortises for the tenons but also means that you don't have to stop the grooves on the stiles as you normally would with frame-and-panel doors. Instead, you just run the grooves the full length of all the frame members.

I usually plane my frame stock $^3/_4$ in. thick and rip the pieces 2 in. wide. Then I groove the inside edge of each piece on the tablesaw. Because $^1/_4$-in. plywood is usually somewhat less than $^1/_4$ in. thick, I don't bother with dado blades. I just cut the groove in two passes with a regular blade raised to $^3/_4$ in. However you cut the groove, it will be helpful to mill extra stock with the frame members for use as test pieces as you seek the setting that will give the panel a snug fit.

Rails get tenons

Next I cut the cheeks of the tenons. Because the tenon length is the same as the groove depth, I leave the tablesaw's blade at the same height I used to cut the groove. I mount the rails onto a simple, shopmade jig for safety and support (see the photo at right).

I cut the tenon shoulders on the tablesaw using the miter gauge. I use the fence as an end stop, which is permissible here (though it isn't in normal crosscutting). That's because I'm not cutting all the way through the piece, so there's no danger of kickback or jamming. You could also use a stop block clamped to an extended fence on your miter gauge.

Size up the panel

I use $^1/_4$-in. cabinet-grade plywood for the panels in most doors like these. For larger or heavier-duty doors, it would be advisable to split the panel with a medial rail or use $^1/_2$-in. plywood and rabbet around the back to produce a $^1/_4$-in. tongue.

When I cut out the panels, I take particular care to ensure that they come out square. Then, when I glue up the frame members around them, I can rely on the panel to make the door square and the glue-up trouble-free.

Dry-assembled door

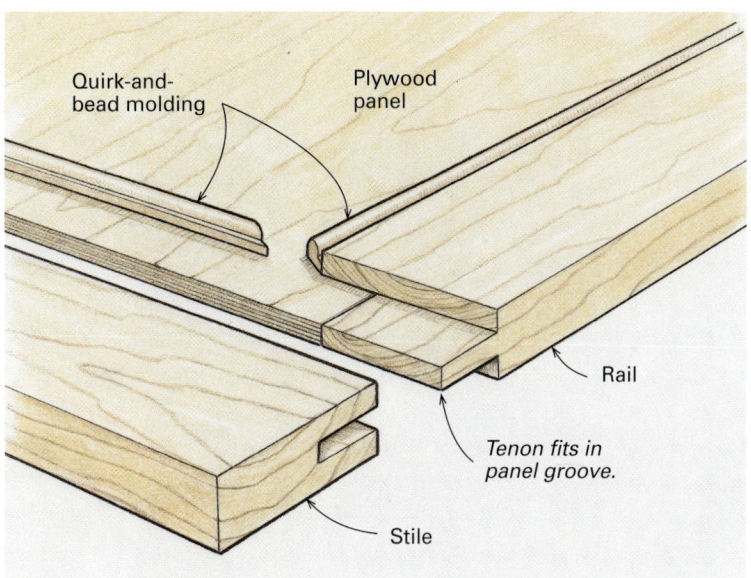

Quirk-and-bead molding

Plywood panel

Rail

Tenon fits in panel groove.

Stile

Tenoning jig from scrap—A stick of pine nailed to a square of medium-density fiberboard makes a jig to produce reliable tenons.

Attending to assembly

When I assemble the doors, I apply glue generously in the grooves and on the tenons. Then I lightly clamp the rails and stiles around the panels. Next I double-check for squareness and clean up the glue squeeze-out. After removing the clamps, I clean up the frame and fair the joints with a sharp block plane.

Beads on every corner—Rodriguez machines all four edges of an extra piece of frame stock to generate molding for a door. For short lengths, use an inverted router; for longer ones, use a router table.

Kerf between the beads to cut their back edge, and then rip the two pieces from the board.

Masking tape supplies all the clamping pressure you need to glue up the molding. The shadow line created by the quirk behind the bead gives a bit of leeway in correcting small mitering errors.

Quirky molding

The quirk-and-bead molding can be produced from excess frame stock with a beading cutter in a router. I bead all four corners of the stock on a router table or simply a router upside down with a fence clamped to the base, as shown in the top left photo. To free the pieces of molding, I cut a kerf down the middle of each edge (see the top right photo) and then rip through the full thickness of the stock.

I cut the miters for the molding on the tablesaw with the miter gauge, but the miters can be cut nearly as fast with a dovetail saw and a block plane for fitting. First I dry-assemble the molding. Then I glue it in with yellow glue and hold it in place with masking tape, as shown in the bottom photo. I close minor misalignments at the miters by pulling the molding away from the frame slightly. The tiny gap created behind the molding won't be noticed—it will read as part of the shadow that gives this simple molding its distinction.

BUILD A HOUSEFUL OF DOORS... WITHOUT COMING UNHINGED

by John Lively

Even before we moved into a Tudor cottage from the 1920s, I knew the doors had to go. Their faceted glass knobs, single flat panels and the dozen coats of gloppy paint definitely did not go with the house. And the doors were ugly to boot.

Soon after we moved in, I was sitting at the drafting table when despair settled in. Building one or two doors was no big deal, but making 16 doors was going to be a prison term of doing the same toilsome tasks over and over.

It was a sad Saturday morning when I told my wife I was going down to the building-supply store to check out the doors. It was even sadder still, when all I found were a lot of raised-panel doors in the Colonial style, a smaller selection of Mediterranean style and hundreds of hollow-core doors whose most exciting feature was a seamless skin of rotary-cut veneer.

By noon, I was back at the drawing board designing much simpler doors with biscuit joints instead of mortise and tenon. My plan was to figure out a strategy that would allow me to make and hang a single door in a weekend or two.

I also wanted to come up with a method of building a door to fit exactly into an

A double row of #20 biscuits, rather than a mortise and tenon, saves time and provides plenty of strength to hold a modest ⅝-in. panel.

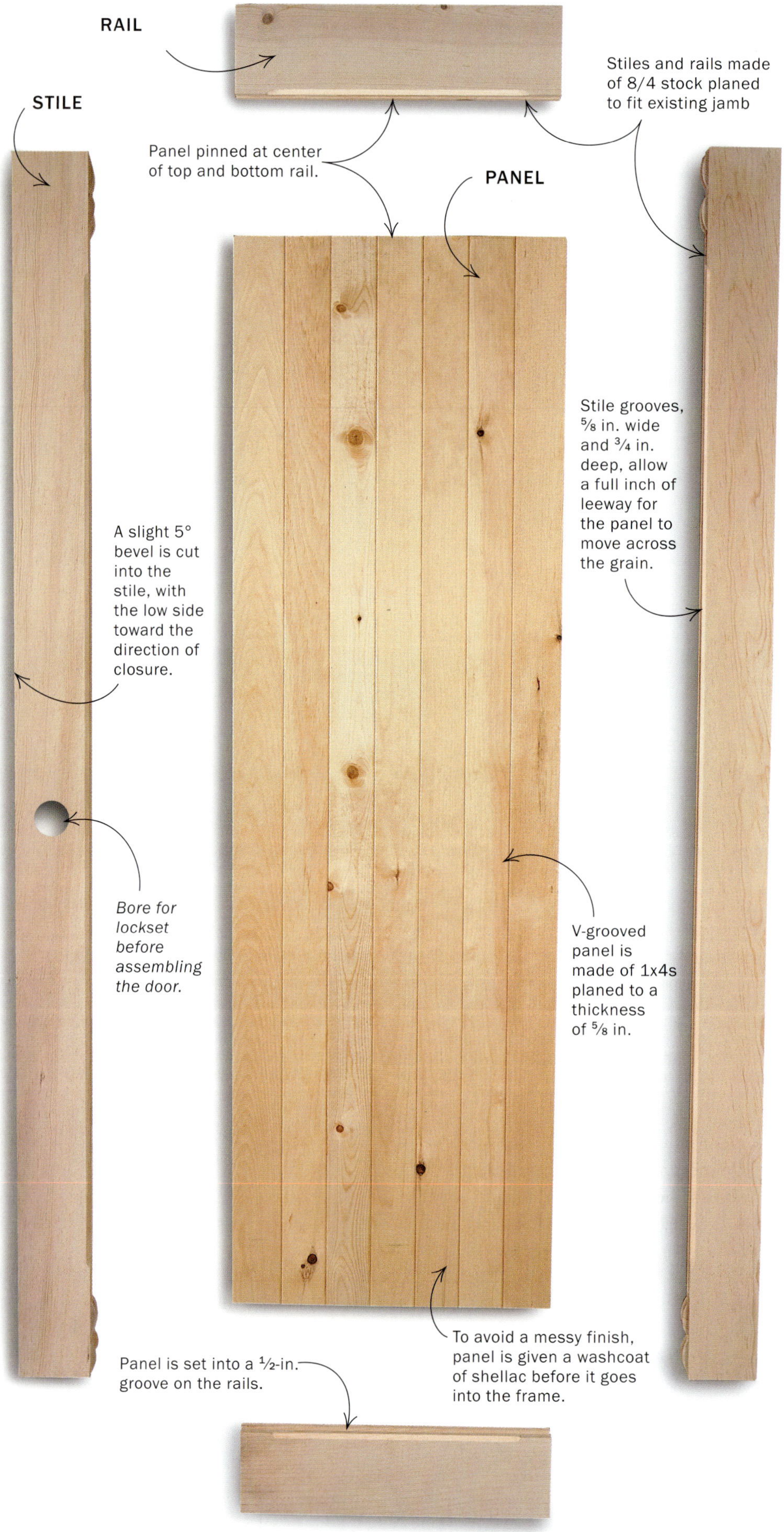

RAIL

STILE

Stiles and rails made of 8/4 stock planed to fit existing jamb

Panel pinned at center of top and bottom rail.

PANEL

A slight 5° bevel is cut into the stile, with the low side toward the direction of closure.

Stile grooves, ⅝ in. wide and ¾ in. deep, allow a full inch of leeway for the panel to move across the grain.

Bore for lockset before assembling the door.

V-grooved panel is made of 1x4s planed to a thickness of ⅝ in.

To avoid a messy finish, panel is given a washcoat of shellac before it goes into the frame.

Panel is set into a ½-in. groove on the rails.

Work out of the jamb

Mark once, cut once. A nickel spacer on the top of the stile and two wedges on the floor hold the stile steady. A centerline is marked alongside the strike plate (above). Laying out the hinge locations with a striking knife (left) is easy work with the stile clamped to the hinges.

existing opening, thus avoiding the tedious and messy task of lugging all my tools out of the basement and into the living space of the house.

Simple elements, major effect

For the sake of straightforward construction, I had to keep the number of elements in each door to a bare minimum—four frame members and one panel. To add interest to the design of the frames, I decided to run stopped chamfers on their inside edges. And on one door, I cut a double-sprung Gothic

arch into the top rail and carved a dogwood blossom. V-grooved 1x4s seemed the right remedy for making such large panels something more than unrelieved expanses of planed wood.

After making the first couple of doors, I was surprised at the visual impact these simple details made.

The doors I made harmonize (to my eye anyway) with the Arts-and-Crafts style of my house. But by fiddling with the details, you can adapt this basic approach to design doors that will work with your house.

Measuring without a rule

When it comes to fitting parts precisely in trim carpentry and cabinet work, a tape measure is about as useful as a baseball bat in a billiard game. A tape measure has all those spaces between the gradations, and in the real world, things seldom fall right on the mark. So you wind up rounding off to the nearest one-sixteenth.

Say you're measuring for a door. The jamb is almost 29¹¹⁄₁₆ in. wide, and you want clearances of ¹⁄₁₆ in. on the hinge side and ³⁄₃₂ in. on the latch side. One stile is a smidge over 4⅝ in. wide, the other just shy of 5¼ in. So to cut the rails to the correct length and make the entire door come out to the right width, you do some eighth-grade arithmetic, then measure and mark the cut. Right? No. Not if you want a precise fit every time. To get that kind of fit, you need a more reliable, more empirical reference. Lots of cabinetmakers and trim carpenters use a two-stick story pole, which, as the name suggests, tells the whole story.

To make one, take some ⅛-in. rippings from the edge of a jointed 2x4, and saw the ends nice and square. When they make contact with the opposite side of the jamb, clamp them together, and mark a line across the one onto the other. Label it "opening width." To figure the other door, all you do is measure from this mark the total clearance you want (in this case, ³⁄₃₂ in.), and make another mark labeled "door width." To determine the exact width of the rails, clamp the stiles together, butt a rail against them, tape the story sticks together at the door-width mark, and measure off the back side of the stiles onto the rail stock.

To get stile length, use a longer pair of sticks in the same way. No squinty-eyed reading of ¹⁄₃₂-in. hash marks, no rounding off to the nearest gradation, no fraction conversions and middle-school math, no trimming to fit later.

A tape measure will get you in the ballpark. A story pole will sink your eightball every time, in one shot.

A door's vertical frame members (stiles) ought to be at least 4½ in. wide, but I prefer them a little wider. The typical back set for a knob location is either 2⅜ in. or 2¾ in., which means to keep knobs centered, stiles should be either 4¾ in. or 5½ in. Also, after boring two big holes in your latch stile, there's not a lot of beef left if you're using narrow stock.

Traditionally, a door's horizontal frame members (rails) are of unequal widths, the bottom rail being considerably wider than the top one. This arrangement offers a maximum amount of wood to be involved in the usual mortise-and-tenon joinery. But with biscuit joinery and modern glues, you can size the rails to your liking. Because you're gluing long grain to cross grain, a 5½-in. rail will provide good strength without enough cross-grain movement to break the joint loose. I get plenty of strength using double rows of biscuits in all four joints.

Keep it in the shop

Adding detail to an unassembled frame. Work moves quickly throughout the shop when you don't have to haul a heavy door from one work area to the next. With the stile clamped securely in the bench, a series of chopping cuts and a smooth pass pares the waste away for a clean mortise that fits every time (above). To prevent tearout when boring for the lockset, drill the beveled edge first, then make two half-depth face bores (left).

Precise dimensioning is key to speed

The greatest aid to speed and efficiency is accuracy in milling. If your stock is milled up square and true, the rest of the work will go smoothly and quickly. But if you mess up on the first part, well, you'll be sorry. So to begin, check and recheck your jointer fence and sawblades for perfect squareness.

Unless you want to move the stops on your door jambs—they'll either be nailed or rabbeted into the jambs—it's best to make your doors the same thickness as the ones you're replacing.

Next edge-joint one edge, rip to width, then edge-joint the sawn edge. Crosscut the rails, but leave them a little long until you determine the final length.

The last step is to plow the grooves in the frame for the panel. I cut grooves $5/8$ in. wide and $1/2$ in. deep across the length of the rails. In the stiles, I cut grooves $3/4$ in. deep, giving the panel a full inch of leeway to move across the grain. Also, I stop the grooves so they don't run far into the joint area.

Before we go on, let's back up a minute. By making a door in your own shop, you can dimension it precisely to the opening before you assemble it. This saves the tedious trial-hanging, unhinging and trimming that carpenters have to endure.

The best measuring method that I've found for this kind of work is described in the box above. So here I'll stick to explaining the standard clearances between door and jamb. Old-time carpenters called it nickel and dime, meaning a skinny $1/16$ in. (dime) clearance at the top and a fat $1/16$ in. (nickel) clearance on each side. My carpen-

Work blocks clamped to a sawhorse hold the door steady while it's dry-fit. Using a polyurethane glue allows plenty of time to make sure that everything is flush, square and aligned. Just remember to mist the biscuits with water to help the glue cure properly.

ter hero Tom Law takes exception to the traditional wisdom.

Law calls for $\frac{1}{16}$ in. on the hinge side, $\frac{3}{32}$ in. on the latch side and $\frac{1}{16}$ in. at the top. Bottom clearances typically call for $\frac{1}{2}$ in. for vinyl floors, $\frac{3}{4}$ in. for hardwoods and $1\frac{1}{2}$ in. for carpet. Once you've measured the opening and have determined the dimensions of the door, you just may have one more problem.

In heaven, square is square,
but on earth, door jambs in older houses seldom are. So check the head jamb for square. If it is square, fine. If it's not and if you're going to build and hang a bunch of doors, it's worth your time to make a big adjustable bevel from two pieces of scrap wood.

Check for squareness, or lack thereof, from the hinge side, and adjust your bevel to the angle made by the hinge-side jamb and the head jamb. If the head jamb is out of square, you can bet the threshold is too.

While you're checking the angle of the threshold, here's a tip that can save re-trimming a door after it's hung: Adjust the bevel to the threshold-to-hinge-side angle. Then holding the bevel tightly against the hinge-side jamb, swing the bevel out across the floor in the angle the door will swing. Any lumps or humps in the floor that will prevent the door from swinging fully open will show up immediately.

Once you've assembled the door to all the other specs, you can transfer the angles from the bevel gauge to the top and bottom of the door and trim to fit in the shop.

Fit the hardware before assembly

Unlike carpenters, you don't have to wrestle a whole door around to mortise for hinges, bore for the lockset and mortise for the latch plate. You can fit all the hardware to the stiles before attaching the rest of the door to them. This makes the work easier, especially if you're nursing a bad case of bench back.

Bevel the edge of the door

The narrow outside edge of the lock-side stile should be beveled to about 5°, with the low side of the bevel toward the direction of closure. Whether you're doing this on your jointer or with a handplane, don't wait until the door is assembled to do it. And don't worry about the bevel interfering with clamping during glue-up. The angle is too slight to throw things off.

Install the lockset

To locate the centers of the lockset bores, hold the lock-side stile against the head jamb using a nickel spacer on top and two wedges underneath. The centerline of the existing latch opening will be the centerline for both lockset bores (see the photo at right).

Follow the template included in the lockset box to find the back-set axis for the face bore and the longitudinal center for the transverse bore. Bore diameters are fairly standard, regardless of brand—1 in. for the latch barrel (transverse bore) and $2\frac{1}{8}$ in. for the knob barrel (face bore).

I use Forstner bits for all the doors. If you bore through the edge first, then run the face bore half-depth on each side, you won't risk the nasty tearout that comes when the 1-in. Forstner breaks through into the larger hole (see the top left photo on p. 83).

Mount the hinges

Laying out the hinge locations for an existing jamb is simple. Again, put a nickel on top of the stile, wedge it from the floor against the head jamb and clamp the stile to the hinges. Use a striking knife to mark the mortises directly off the hinge leaves.

Then back in the shop, with the stile in a vise, you can cut the mortises in whatever fashion you prefer, knowing that you won't have to jigger the fit when you hang the door.

The high craft of door hanging

In the traditional sense, door hanging is a mystery you don't have to worry about. That's because, if you've followed the method described here, you've already done it. You have actually incorporated hanging the door into the very process of making the door.

So after you have applied the finish, mounted the hinges and installed the lockset, all that's left is to slide the hinge pins home and shut the door. Click.

A door that travels well. The author uses the same door design for a clean look in the master bedroom.

HANGING A CABINET DOOR

by Philip C. Lowe

Begin with the bottom. This edge, planed clean and square, becomes the reference point for the fitting and hanging to follow.

Dry-fit with $\frac{1}{16}$-in. shims under the door. Check and adjust the hinge stile next and the top after that. The joint between the doors is the last edge to be fit.

Score hinge locations with the layout knife. No shop should be without this knife; it provides a precision unmatched by a pencil or a scratch awl.

Set the marking gauge for the thinnest part of the leaf. With extruded hinges, an even spacing between the two leaves will be just right if the hinges are mortised to the depth of the thinnest part of the hinge.

It's the simple pleasures that make my day. Fabricating a pair of doors, mortising them for good-quality butt hinges and then installing the doors so they function without binding all add up to one of those simple pleasures in furnituremaking—a door that's hung right.

Real technological advances have been made in hinges in the past 20 years. For cabinetwork, you can choose butt hinges of stamped sheet brass bent around a steel pin, hinges of extruded material milled to shape and fitted with either fixed or loose pins,

cast hinges milled with stops, hinges with one leaf longer than the other, or hinges with and without finials. For more on these choices and where you can get them. All of them, though, depend on careful installation for smooth operation.

Choose before you build

The best time to select hinges for any project is in the design phase. Here are some of the questions you should ask:

• Is the hinge strong enough to support the weight of the door?

Door mortises

Mortising into the door stile—The author begins the mortising process by cutting a sawkerf just shy of his knife line.

Self-centering bit finds the hole. This bit, with the hinge held firmly where it belongs, locates pilot holes for the screws.

Feather cuts against the grain—Striking these chisel blows first makes removing the waste easier.

Paring strokes remove the waste. By working to a scribed line, the author cuts a clean mortise in a few easy strokes.

Final chops to size—This last chisel cut on the ends of the mortise for the door stile will make a snug fit for the hinge.

- Where and how will the hinges be installed?

- How many hinges do you need?

- How thick is the material the hinges will be set into?

- What size screws will you need to secure the hinges?

- Will those screws have enough holding power?

For casework, like the cabinet shown in the photo on p. 92, you will have to decide whether you want the doors to have an overlay or an inset design (meaning that they fit within the frame of the case, as I did with this one). With an inset design, the thickness of the door will determine the size of the hinge. With an overlay design, the thickness of the case, or face frame, will dictate the width of the hinge leaf. Butt-hinge sizes are specified by their length and their width in the open position, which includes the width of both leaves plus the knuckle.

Fit the door on three sides first

A pair of inset doors will function well only if they fit the opening of the case with enough clearance not to bind; $^1/_{16}$ in. on all sides is ideal for most cabinet doors. After the doors are assembled (I make them a little oversized), I fit them to the case, leaving the two edges that meet in the middle. Those are trimmed later.

I start by planing the bottom of the door in both directions to avoid tearout on the edges of the stiles (see the right photo on p. 86). I find or make some $^1/_{16}$-in. shims, place them on the case bottom and set the door on top of them to check the fit, as shown in the top photo on p. 87. I pay attention to the stile on the hinge side. If it doesn't meet the side of the case squarely, I can do one of two things: either plane the edge of the door to follow the line of the case or, if that would take off too much of the stile, plane the bottom of the door on one side or the other to square up the fit. Once the bottom and hinge edges look good, I plane the top edge as necessary to

maintain a consistent $^1/_{16}$-in. gap along the width of the door.

Locating the hinges on the door

The placement of the hinge will vary with the design of the door. I usually align the top of the upper hinge and the bottom of the lower hinge with the inside lines of the top and bottom rails. But with these doors, I thought the upper hinge would look better centered on the small top panels.

Using a square and a knife, I scribe lines on the edge of the stile to indicate the top of the upper hinge and the bottom of the lower hinge (see the bottom left photo on p. 87). With the door held in a vise, I place each hinge on the edge of the door, tight to the scribed lines, and then use the knife to mark the corner at the other end of each hinge. I transfer those marks with a square across the edge of the stile.

At this point, for a good custom fit, I usually number each hinge and door so I won't get any of the hinges mixed up later (you'll find minor variations even in hinges that look identical). I use a pencil to extend the scribed lines to the face of the door. These lines give start and stop marks that keep me from scratching in a line past where the mortise will be cut. I set a marking gauge to the thickness of the hinge leaf (see the bottom right photo on p. 87) and scribe a line along the face of the door between the two pencil marks.

Cutting the mortises in the door

As long as the width of the hinge leaf is the same or even a little less than the thickness of the door stile, I mortise all the way across the edge. I use a dovetail saw to make a relief cut about $^1/_{16}$ in. away from the scribed lines, down to the depth of the marking-gauge line, as shown in the photos on the facing page. With a wide chisel, I chop a series of feather cuts across the edge of the stile, taking care not to go below the scribed line. Then I pare away the waste. For the final depth cut, I place the chisel in the marking-gauge line, flat side down, and cut across the stile. To finish, I place the chisel vertically into the scribed knife lines at the

Case mortises

With the door in place, mark the hinge locations for the case. After the doors are fit and hinged, the author puts them back into the cabinet and scribes the top and bottom locations with the layout knife.

Score and clean out the mortises with a chisel. Sharp tools make this job quick and accurate.

Mortising into the case—The author follows the same procedures as he did for the door-stile mortises. He starts with scribed knife lines (left) and follows that with relief cuts made with the backsaw (right).

Final fitting

Getting the center gap right—Mark the overlap of one door to the other (left). Get a precise measurement of that overlap (above). To end up with a ⅟₁₆-in. gap between the two doors, divide the overlap distance by two, add ⅟₃₂ in. and remove that amount from the first door. Trim the second door to fit.

top and bottom of each hinge and chop out the little bit of remaining waste.

After the mortises are cut, I screw the hinges to the stiles. I find a self-centering bit is a big help (see the bottom left photo on p. 88). Some people like to start with just one screw per hinge leaf to check the fit. I prefer to start with at least two, because the door will sometimes pivot and rack on one screw. If the job feels like it's going well, I'll add all the screws.

Marking and cutting the case

I set the door back in the case, on top of the shims. Then I mark the top and bottom of each hinge on the inside corner edge of the case side with the layout knife, as shown in the top left photo on the facing page. Again, using a square and a knife, I scribe the lines into the case as far as the hinge leaf needs to

go for the door face to sit flush with the front of the case (see the bottom left photo on the facing page).

The marking gauge should still be set for the thickness of the hinge. I scribe that line into the front edge of the case, reset the gauge to the width of the hinge leaf and scribe that line parallel to the front edge of the case. If the size of the cabinet will allow it, I place the case on its side on my workbench. That makes it easier to do the work that follows.

With a dovetail saw, I make relief cuts ⅟₁₆ in. inside the finished top and bottom scribed lines, as shown in the top right photo. I hold the saw on a slight diagonal to stop the cut at the back and bottom lines of the mortise. I define the back line of the mortise with some firm chisel strikes (see the top right photo on the facing page). Just as I did with the door, I stay $^1/_{16}$ in. away from the outside lines, chop feather cuts down to the line made by the marking gauge, and relieve the waste with the flat of the chisel. After that, I finish the mortise by chiseling out the small bits of waste left along the outside lines.

Hanging the doors

I place a few battens (the same thickness as the side of the case) on the workbench to support the door and fit the hinge leaves into the mortises. Just as I did with the doors, I bore holes with a centering bit, pilot bit and a bit for the screw shank. Keep in mind that you may need to use a shorter screw in the side of the case. I secure the doors in place. Then I put the case in an upright position so the doors can swing freely.

Final fitting

The last adjustment needs to be made at the joint where the two doors meet (see the photos on p. 91). The object is to remove the same amount of material from each door and to end up with a $^1/_{16}$-in. gap in the middle. So with the doors closed and one overlapping the other, I mark and measure the overlap, divide that by two and add $^1/_{32}$ in. That tells me how much to remove from the first edge.

Then I mark that dimension in pencil along the stile of the first door, move it to the vise and plane to that line. I secure the door in its place, close it in position, overlapping the other door, and mark a pencil line at the joint. I add another $^1/_{16}$ in. to that line, move the door to the vise and plane to the finished line. I like to put a slight bevel to this inside edge, removing a little more material from the back side, so that the doors clear one another more easily when they open and close.

I hang the door and check that the spacing is consistent top to bottom, making any final adjustments before the final sanding and finishing stages. At this point, it doesn't hurt to take a moment to step back and appreciate the result of your efforts.

A finished fit—Gaps around doors are almost perfectly consistent in this mahogany and Sitka spruce cabinet.

GLAZING CABINET DOORS

by Tony Konovaloff

I've opened a lot of glass doors on finely crafted cabinets and cringed. The joints are tight, the finish is fine, but the glass is held in place by methods that look, at least to my eye, crude. I've seen big, clunky strips held in place by #8 screws, badly done putty and perhaps worst of all, vinyl strips screwed or even stapled to the door frame.

What looks much better is glass set in a relatively deep rabbet in the frame and held in place with beveled strips of wood on the back side of the door. The strips function like quarter-round molding, but the profile is more refined. The strips, which are easy to make, are fastened to the shoulder of the rabbet with brass escutcheon pins. Should the glass need to be replaced, the strips easily pop off and can be reused.

Holding glass in a door this way is nothing new. It's an old technique that works because it's simple and practical, and it looks good whether the door is open or closed.

Designing for glass

With glass-front cabinets, the focus is not on the furniture but on what's inside it. Before you begin making the cabinet, think about how a glass front will affect the design and construction. For instance, everything is now visible, so the layout and fit of the joints on the inside of the cabinet are as important as those on the outside.

Glass thickness and temper

Standard window glass is only $3/32$ in. thick, and I use it almost exclusively. It's called

Glass adds a whole new dimension to a cabinet. The inside is as important as the outside. The thin beveled strips holding the glass to the back of these doors looks good from either side.

93

Building the frame

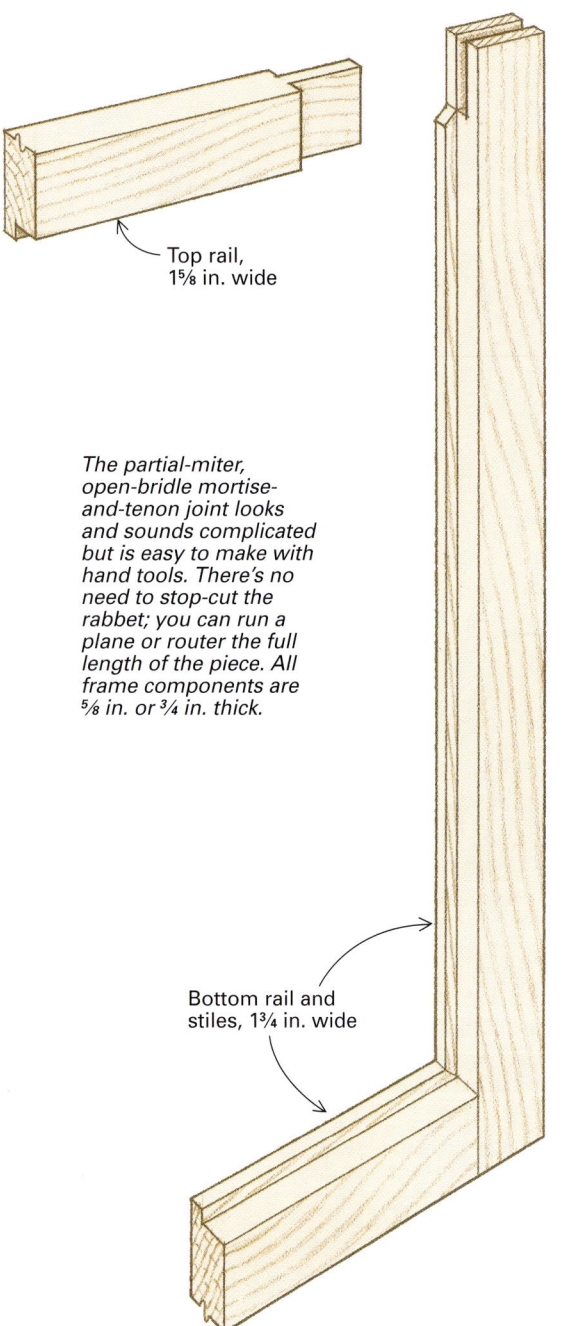

Top rail,
1⅝ in. wide

The partial-miter,
open-bridle mortise-
and-tenon joint looks
and sounds complicated
but is easy to make with
hand tools. There's no
need to stop-cut the
rabbet; you can run a
plane or router the full
length of the piece. All
frame components are
⅝ in. or ¾ in. thick.

Bottom rail and
stiles, 1¾ in. wide

single-thickness float glass, and I buy it cut
to order at a local glass shop. When safety is
a factor (when the glass will be near the
floor in a household with children, for
example), I use tempered glass. The thinnest
readily available size of tempered glass is
⅛ in., and it has to be special-ordered (see
the story on p. 99).

I wouldn't use beveled strips where the
glass is thicker than 1/8 in. because the rails
and the stiles must be beefed up to accommodate the glass and the larger strips.
Unless the cabinet is really large, the whole
thing probably will look clumsy.

Glass weighs about three times as much
as wood. But the weight of a simple door
glazed with ³⁄₃₂-in. or ⅛-in. glass is roughly
the same as that of a similar wooden panel
door because the glass is so much thinner.
There's no need to consider special hinges
or hardware.

Glass color and wood choice
Standard float glass, sometimes called soda-
lime float glass, has a slight green tinge (see
the photo on p. 99). The effect is more
noticeable as the thickness of the glass
increases, and it can alter the color of the
wood behind it. Sometimes the effect can be
pleasing, and sometimes it's not. Test it by
looking at wood samples through the glass
you intend to use.

Dimensions and construction of frames
When sizing the cabinet-door frames, keep
in mind that the clear front affects the
apparent widths of the frame pieces. The
same size frame you'd use for a wooden
panel front looks too heavy with glass.

When I make a medium-sized cabinet
door (something like 15 in. wide by 24 in.
tall), the frame pieces are ⅝ in. or ¾ in.
thick, depending on the thickness of the
glass. I make the bottom rail and the stiles
1¾ in. wide, with the top rail ⅛ in. narrower. The rabbet depth is two-thirds the thickness of the frame.

I join my frames with a partial-miter,
open-bridle mortise and tenon. It's a long-
winded name for something quite simple
(see the drawing above). It's an old molding
joint that saves the trouble of stop-cutting
the rabbets. The joint is quick and easy to

Vise-mounted bench

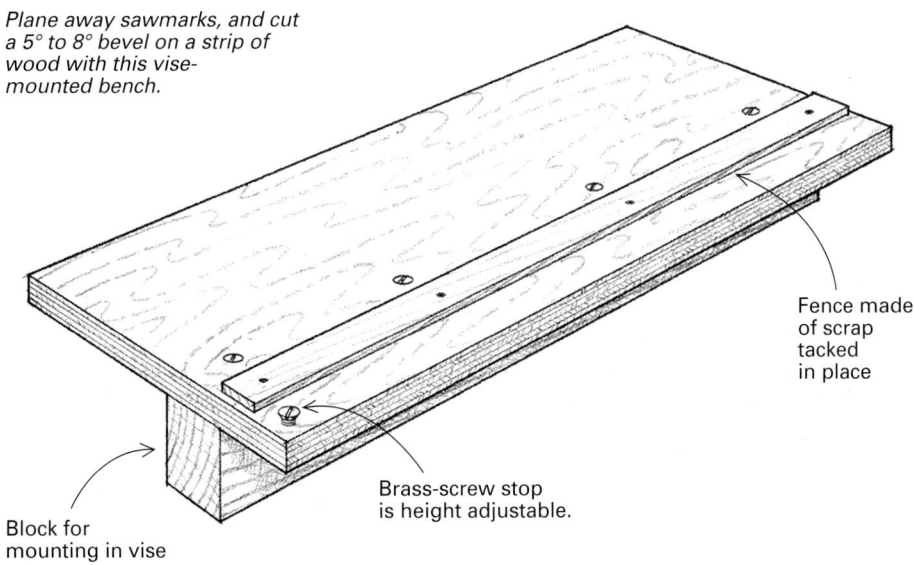

Plane away sawmarks, and cut a 5° to 8° bevel on a strip of wood with this vise-mounted bench.

Fence made of scrap tacked in place

Brass-screw stop is height adjustable.

Block for mounting in vise

do with hand tools (which are all I use), because you can cut the joint first and then run the rabbet the full length of the piece. It's also an attractive joint.

Another way to join the frames is to glue up a doweled (or biscuited) frame and run a rabbet around the inside with a router, squaring up the corners with a chisel. It really doesn't matter how the frames are made as long as you plan for the rabbet.

Installing the glass

When the doors are made but not finished, I take them to the local glass shop to have the glass fitted. A good slip fit is desirable for the glass—if it's loose in the frame, it may rattle when a truck drives by. There's no need to allow for movement in either the wood or the glass in a medium-sized door.

If the glass is too snug in the frame, adjust the fit with a rabbet plane and a bull-nose rabbet plane. If the glass is a little small, you can shim out the rabbets with thin slivers of wood. Nothing will show once the beveled strips are in place

Once the glass fits correctly, I turn my attention back to the door. I fit it to the carcase and install the hinges and catches. Then I finish the door (inside and out) and set it aside.

Fitting the beveled strips

The beveled strips are sized so that when they're installed, they will stand slightly proud of the frame and be a little narrower than the rabbet (see the drawing on p. 97). The strips are not rectangular in section—they bevel about 5° to 8° (see the bottom right photo on p. 96). This makes them less visible from the outside.

I rip the strips from long scraps of the same wood as the frame. I plane all four sides (including the bevel) on a small vise-mounted bench I built for handling small pieces (see the top photo on p. 96 and the drawing above). It has an adjustable stop made from a brass screw and a light fence tacked on to hold the strips for planing. Then I lightly chamfer all the edges with a small spokeshave (see the bottom left photo on p. 96).

Using the mini-bench—A screw keeps the strip in place while the author planes a 5° to 8° bevel.

Chamfering the beveled strips relieves any sharp edges.

The strip on the left is ready to install. The bevel and chamfers, though small, are obvious when compared to the rectangular strip on the right.

When the finish on the door is dry, I lay it on the bench, set the glass in the rabbet, and fit the strips: first the top and bottom strips and then the sides. I cut them a little long with a backsaw and then pare them to fit with a chisel (see the photo at right). Because of the bevel, the side pieces aren't cut at a right angle. The best way to fit them is by paring away a little at a time. Once the strips are fitted, I lightly file the corners to match the chamfer on the other pieces.

Fastening the strips

I prefer escutcheon pins over brads for holding the strips in place. I like the look of the brass head, and the pins make a more secure fastening. I use #18 escutcheon pins, $5/8$ in. long.

With the strips fitted in place, I mark the locations of the escutcheon pins every 4 in. to 5 in. I remove the strips and drill the shank holes for a push fit. I use a #53 (0.059 in.) or #54 drill (0.055 in.), depending on the wood. Check the fit in a piece of scrap to be sure. I drill the holes at right angles to the bevel and clean up both sides of the hole by turning a small countersink a few times by hand (see the bottom photo on p. 98).

I put the escutcheon pins partway in the shank holes in the strips and put the strips back in place on the glass. Holding the strip firmly in place, I lightly tap each pin to mark the frame for the pilot holes. After removing the strips and the glass, I use the marks in the frame as centers for drilling the pilot holes. I use a #55 drill (0.052) for a hammer fit, and I drill at about 5° off the perpendicular—the amount of the bevel.

Everything is ready for final assembly, but first I finish both the strips and the inside of the cabinet with paste wax.

Final assembly

Before installing the glass, I clean it one last time. I put it back in the frame, put the strips in place and protect the glass with a piece of cardboard cut from a cereal box. I set the escutcheon pins with a 3-oz. Warrington hammer; it's light and narrow, perfect for such delicate work (see the photo

Use a chisel to pare the ends of the strips to fit after cutting them a little long with a backsaw.

Attaching the beveled strips ⎯⎯⎯⎯

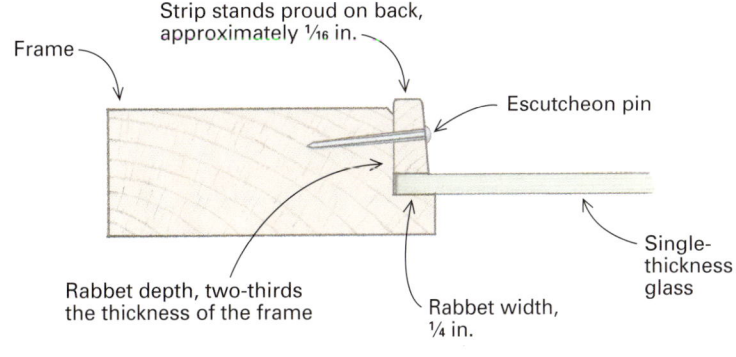

Frame

Strip stands proud on back, approximately 1/16 in.

Escutcheon pin

Rabbet depth, two-thirds the thickness of the frame

Rabbet width, 1/4 in.

Single-thickness glass

Protect the glass with cardboard, and carefully use a light hammer when setting the escutcheon pins.

Clean up both sides of the escutcheon-pin shank holes by hand-turning a small countersink.

above). Don't try to drive the pins in one blow—take it slowly. Be careful not to hit the strips, or they'll be marred by the hammer.

If an escutcheon pin goes into the frame too easily because the diameter of the pilot hole is a little too big or the hole too deep, you can tighten it up by bending the pin. Just hit it with the other end of a Warrington hammer to put in a slight curve. When you put the pin back in the pilot hole, it'll snug up nicely.

Because I've already fit and finished the door, all that's left is to mount it in the cabinet. After this is done, I install a small riser in each door opening to support the doors when closed. Risers are pieces of wood, ¼ in. by ¼ in. by ⅜ in. long, mortised into the cabinet bottom on the catch side. The block goes in end grain up and is filed down until its height equals the gap between the carcase and the door (about the thickness of a business card). The door rests lightly on the riser and opens and closes freely.

Getting clear on glass

by Aimé Fraser

People who work with glass have their own language, and the terms don't necessarily coincide with common usage. As glass formulations and manufacturing change, so do the words. Here's a partial list to make it easier to talk with your glazier.

Plate glass

These days, plate glass is a generic term for sheet glass, but it has a more specific meaning to glaziers. To them, it refers to sheet goods produced by running molten glass through rollers and then lapping and polishing it on both sides. This is the way most glass was made prior to the 1960s, but it is a labor-intensive process. Plate glass is used now only for high-quality optical glass.

Float glass

About 30 years ago, a new manufacturing process was perfected that fully automated the production of flat and virtually distortion-free glass. A plant easily can manufacture a nearly perfect sheet of glass 4 ft. wide and a quarter of a mile long. Today, the bulk of commonly available glass is produced this way.

The whole process takes place in a giant oven. Molten glass is poured onto a pool of molten tin, where it levels itself out. It cools slightly and is slid off the tin and into an annealing oven. From there, it is reheated to just below the melting point and then cooled slowly to relieve internal stresses. When annealed glass breaks, it breaks into large, irregular sharp shards.

Tempered glass

It is possible to temper glass and alter its breaking characteristics so that it breaks into small, relatively harmless pieces. In the bargain, the glass is strengthened. The downside is that once tempered, the glass cannot be drilled, cut or even nicked without shattering into tiny pieces.

Tempered glass starts as annealed glass that is cut and machined to its finished dimensions. It's put into the oven and heated once more, almost to the melting point. Then it's quickly cooled on one side by jets of chilled air, which causes rapid hardening of the glass on that side; the other side is still red hot. This builds a great deal of stress into the glass, so when it breaks, it shatters into thousands of pieces. Each one is the size of the area cooled by one jet.

On thick glass, this process causes no distortion. But it can cause thinner or smaller pieces of glass to curl like a potato chip. For this reason, glass less than $\frac{1}{8}$ in. thick is usually tempered chemically. It's not as strong as heat-tempered glass, and it breaks into larger pieces.

Leaded glass

The color of the glass is determined by the mineral content of the sand it's made from. Each sand quarry produces glass of a slightly different color, which can be altered by the addition or extraction of various mineral oxides. The green color of common glass is from iron oxide. When this mineral is removed, the glass has almost no color (see the

Double-thickness soda-lime float glass (top) has a slightly green tinge. Water-white glass of the same thickness (bottom) has almost no color.

photo above). The addition of lead will further enhance clarity, but leaded glass cannot be produced by the float method. It must be lapped and polished; however, the process does produce optical-quality glass for lenses and prisms.

Single-thickness glass

Glass is manufactured in a variety of thicknesses from 0.0394 in. (1mm) up to several inches. Most glass is $\frac{3}{32}$ in. thick. The industry has designated this single thickness, whether or not it has been tempered.

Double-thickness glass

For some reason, $\frac{1}{8}$-in.-thick glass is commonly known as double thickness, even though this glass is only $\frac{1}{32}$ in. thicker than single-thickness glass.

FIVE

Hinges and Locks

Hinges and locks are deceptive. They're small, so we think of installing them as no big deal. But a half dozen half-mortise locks fitted to drawers on a large cabinet will take a substantial portion of time, certainly more than a 9 to 5 workday. Butt hinges take less time, but still are nothing to sniff at to get right.

There is a fine art to installing hardware that requires a number of skills and, with the more complex parts, a fair amount of patience. First, it's one of the few times woodworkers have to work with another material: metal. Many simply try to cut the wood around the metal, and, finding out that many hinges aren't exactly square, straight, or perfect, end up with a compromised fit. More experienced woodworkers realize that metal can be shaped as well. In some limited circumstances, the solution can be to fit the hinge to the mortise. Metal files will straighten the edge of a badly cast brass hinge leaf very quickly.

Hardware often involves a great number of steps for installation. This makes it essential to get the proverbial ducks in a row before starting. There is a definite order to the steps for fitting a lock that risks headaches if broken. Like the game of chess, you win only when you can see ahead several moves. The trick for an amateur is simply to remember the steps. Keeping the book open on the workbench is not considered cheating, but rather a wise way to conserve hot language by not making mistakes.

In fact, fitting hinges can be among the most enjoyable jobs in woodworking. Most of the work requires that you sit down at the bench, and pull out small chisels, drills, a marking knife, and not much more. The work goes along slowly, without screaming tools, blowing dust, or volatile finishes wafting up your nose. You can even listen to the radio, though talk shows tend to loosen your concentration by sending your mind on tangents. For the precision work needed to get a mortise lock in place evenly and working, distractions can be fatal.

INSTALLING KNIFE HINGES

by Gary Rogowski

Installing knife hinges well means getting the door flush with the case and getting a consistent reveal all around the door. The author achieves a consistent reveal by setting scrap pieces of plastic laminate between the door and carcase and then marking and trimming the door accordingly.

Knife hinges are a sweet finale to a piece of cabinetry. They have a simple, subtle beauty. Just a small semicircle of brass is all that shows with the door closed, letting the lines of the furniture and the figure of the wood take center stage. Knife hinges also are tremendously strong and almost totally resistant to sagging, making them the hinges of choice wherever a narrow, consistent reveal around a door is important.

Knife hinges are strong because of the orientation of their leaves. Their leaves are mortised flush to the horizontal surfaces of the door and the carcase. The forces of gravity and leverage acting on the hinge put shearing forces on the screws. In other words, for the door to fall off its hinges, or even sag, the screws would have to shear, or the door frame or carcase would have to be destroyed. Not so with butt hinges, where gravity and leverage exert forces of tension on the screws. Over time, this causes the door to sag and tends to pull the screws out of their holes.

Despite their advantages, knife hinges have gotten a bad rap for being notoriously difficult to install. They are less forgiving of sloppiness, but with a little extra care in layout and mortising, knife hinges are no more difficult to install than butt hinges.

Don't buy inexpensive hinges

A number of different types and brands of knife hinges are available, but only one brand I know of is really worth considering. Avoid hinges that are made from stamped steel, have riveted pins (making them inseparable and, therefore, next to impossible to install accurately) or are finished poorly. The good ones are made by Larry and Faye Brusso and are available through many woodworking catalogs or directly from Larry and Faye Brusso Co. Inc. (4865 Highland Road, Suite J, Waterford, Mich. 48328; 810-674-8458).

Brusso hinges consist of two machined and polished brass leaves, each about $\frac{1}{8}$ in. thick, countersunk for screws (see the photo below). The leaves, which come apart, pivot on a short pin and are separated by a single washer. They come in many sizes, but there are just two basic types of knife hinges: straight and L-shaped.

The straight knife hinge is used in situations where the top and bottom of the carcase extend over the door frame, and the door frame covers the carcase sides.

The L-shaped knife hinge is used on full inset doors. The short leg of the hinge, into which the pivot pin is set, moves the pivot point away from the carcase so that the door

Knife hinges aren't all created equal. The hinges on the left and right are stamped steel with faux finishes and have a riveted pivot pin, making them inseparable. Because you can't take them apart, it's nearly impossible to install this type of knife hinge with any accuracy. The machined and polished brass hinge in the center is a Brusso hinge. It's thicker and therefore stronger; the hinge leaves come apart, making it much easier to install; and, because it's machined to precise tolerances, the hinge moves smoothly, unlike the two stamped hinges here which tended to bind.

Many varieties of plastic laminate are conveniently the same thickness as the knife-hinge's washer. Cardboard and other materials can also be used as shims if you don't have ready access to scraps of laminate.

Pencil marks establish limits for marking-gauge line. Using a laminate shim against the carcase wall to set the hinge-stile reveal, the author marks the hinge-leaf end and the edge of the short leg of the "L." This keeps him from accidentally scratching the marking gauge line beyond the hinge and leaving a sloppy layout line.

can swing clear of the carcase side without binding. Brusso also offers an L-shaped hinge (L-39) with an extra long short leg for use in cabinets where the door must clear a protruding corner post to open fully.

Accurate placement is key to success

Laying out the mortises for either type of knife hinge involves essentially the same steps. Layout is the most critical part of setting them. Installed correctly, knife hinges will hold a door true to the face of the carcase and establish a consistent reveal between the door and the carcase sides all the way around. The key to achieving both of these goals is accurate placement of the hinge leaves. This comes down to a precise hinge setback in both the carcase and door and shimming the door hinge against the carcase wall to set the reveal. The photos accompanying this article show how to do this and how to hang a cabinet door using a set of L-shaped knife hinges, the more commonly used type of knife hinges.

Hanging a door using knife hinges begins with making sure the dry-assembled carcase's face is flat and square. Before glu-

Scratch a marking gauge line from pencil mark to pencil mark. Take care not to let the gauge run with the grain.

Knife mark the end of the hinge leaf and the inside edge of the "L," and then erase the pencil lines. With the marking-gauge line establishing the front edge of the hinge, you've got an accurate starting point from which to mark adjacent lines. Position the hinge leaf on the marking-gauge line, and be careful not to let the hinge move as you mark end and edge.

ing up the carcase, lay out the two carcase hinge mortises, disassemble the carcase and then rout and pare the hinge mortises (see the photos on the facing page and the top photo at right). Glue-up the carcase, and then let the glue dry, checking again to make sure the carcase is square across its opening. Plane or sand the face of the carcase flat.

Doors should fit snugly

The door should be built to fit snugly in the carcase opening. Trim the door, so it just fits in the opening with shims along the bottom rail and the hinge stile. The shims should be the same thickness as the washer that separates the two leaves of the hinge (leave the handle stile and top rail tight for now). At this point, I have mortises in the carcase and can cut the mortise in the bottom of the door. I lay it out and cut it in much the same way as I did in the carcase (see the second photo from the top at right).

The next step is to put hinge leaves into their mortises. A friction fit should keep them in, but you can tape them in if you like. Put the door into the carcase opening with the bottom hinge connected. Check and mark the reveal again on the bottom, hinge-stile side and on the top, as necessary. Plane or sand the door's edge to get the reveal right on these three sides. Then lay out and mortise for the top door hinge. Screw the carcase hinge leaves and the bottom door-hinge leaf into place, but be sure to drill and cut the threads first by screwing steel screws of the same size into the screw holes. This keeps the brass heads of the screws that come with the hinges from marring or stripping.

The final fitting of the door will be done with both hinges in place but left unscrewed. Hold the top door-hinge leaf on its mating leaf in the carcase while you set the door into the lower hinge pin. Slide the top of the door onto the door-hinge leaf (see the bottom right photo on p. 106). Close the door, and check and mark the handle-stile reveal (see the photo on p. 102). Open the door, slide it off, plane or

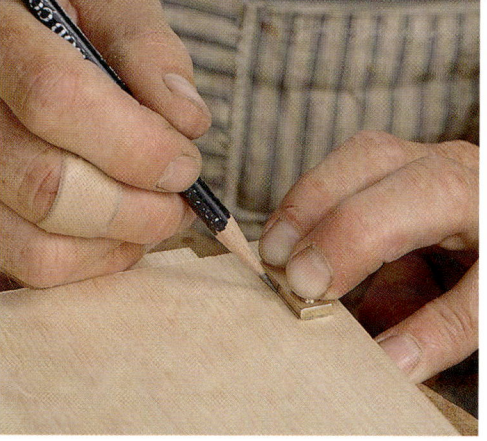

Pencil mark the back of the hinge leaf. This is just a rough approximation to keep you safely within bounds when routing the hinge mortise. You'll mark the actual back edge of the hinge later.

Rout out the bulk of the hinge mortise using a small bit. The author uses a ³⁄₁₆-in. bit set for the thickness of the hinge leaf and stays well away from the knife marks and pencil mark defining the mortise.

Pare the front wall of the hinge mortise carefully, taking the mortise just to the knife mark.

Lean up any roughness on the back wall of the mortise, but stay well away from pencil line.

Knife mark the back edge of the hinge mortise, tilting the hinge leaf into the mortise and holding it tightly against the front wall of the mortise. Then pare carefully to this knife line, checking constantly to see if the hinge leaf will fit. Once it fits, that mortise is done. The procedure is the same for all four mortises.

Routing a hinge mortise in the cabinet door's thin bottom edge would be a tippy proposition without any added support. The author's solution is to clamp a board to the door, level with its edge, to provide a wider platform for the router's base. Clamp pads (held in place with spring clamps) keep the C-clamps from damaging the door frame.

Predrilling the hinge-leaf screwholes tight up against the carcase's side would be impossible with a power drill or even a corner brace: the holes are just too close to the side. A Yankee drill is able to get close enough, though. A piece of cardboard keeps the side of the carcase from being marred by the drill.

sand the door's edge to get an even reveal all the way around and reinstall the door. The door-handle stile can be trimmed back at a slight angle to provide clearance for the door as it swings past the case.

What if it's not perfect?

All is not necessarily lost if the fit is less than perfect. Hinges that are too deep can be shimmed in the mortises. If the leaves aren't deep enough, then you can rout or pare the door mortises a little deeper. Case mortises are tougher to get to, but with a router plane or a swan-neck chisel, you can remove material from them as well.

If it's just a little bit off, a door that's not flush with its carcase can be planed or sanded to match the case. For more serious adjustments, you can shift a hinge mortise's location by gluing in carefully matched pieces of scrap and remortising. If it's just a screw that's out of place, you can usually drill out the holes, fill them with sections of dowel and redrill.

To do final fit of the door, set the door in place and the bottom hinge connected, slide the door onto the top hinge. Friction should hold the top carcase hinge leaf in place, but tape adds a measure of security.

HANGING BUTT HINGES

by Stephen Lamont

Several years ago, I moved to Devon, England, with my wife and son to study with an excellent craftsman and teacher named Christopher Faulkner. He taught me the basics of furnituremaking, one by one. I remember spending hours painstakingly cutting the mortises for my first set of butt hinges on a tool cabinet that I still use.

As with most of what I learned back then, the process of installing those hinges was pretty exciting. Yet, in some ways, it's even more so now because of some of the unusual design details that have come up in my work. Practical or esthetic considerations sometimes lead to different approaches to installing hinges.

Hanging doors in front of drawers

I received a commission a few years ago to build a stereo cabinet. The clients had a collection of audio tapes and compact discs, and they wanted room for more. So I had to design a bank of drawers within the cabinet, behind the doors. With a conventional butt-hinge installation, the inset door would have to open a full 180° for the drawers to clear the hinge stile. That would make the simple task of pulling out a tape or compact disc impractical and inconvenient.

My solution to this problem was to bevel both the door stile and the mating surface of the cabinet. It's the location of the hinge pin that determines the path of a swinging door. The bevels effectively moved the hinge pin away from the path of the drawer so that the door could swing clear of it when opened only a bit more than 90°, as shown in the photo at right.

A drawer behind a door

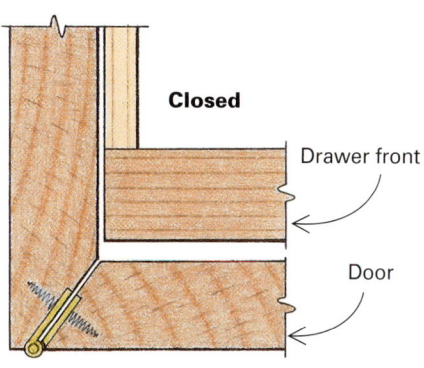

Closed

Drawer front

Door

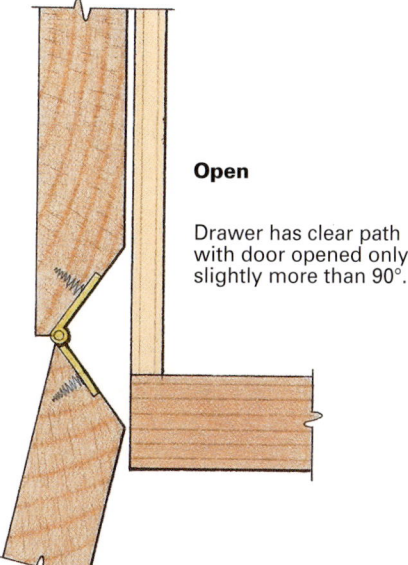

Open

Drawer has clear path with door opened only slightly more than 90°.

Doors set in from the cabinet face

Sometimes, the design of a cabinet will require that the doors be set back from the front face of the carcase. In such cases, you could mortise the hinge into the carcase as you would if the door were flush with the front. This locates the pin all the way out to the front edge of the carcase, so the door swings freely and opens all the way. But doing that would make the hinge look unsightly; too much of the leaf would be exposed, as shown in the drawing below left.

A more attractive solution is one I learned from a book by Ernest Joyce, *The Technique of Furniture Making* (published as *Encyclopedia of Furniture Making* in the United States by Sterling Publishing Co., New York, N.Y.). It's a little complicated and more difficult to cut the mortise because you have to cut it in at an angle. The key here is to make sure the pivot point of the hinge is in line with the front of the door. Mortise the knuckle entirely into the door stile at the front, and mortise the leaves equally into the edge of the door stile and the cabinet side at the back, as shown in the drawing below right.

There's one drawback to this method: It limits the door travel. Depending on how far back the door is hung, its face will bind on the inside front edge of the cabinet. And because the door travel is restricted, this application would not work with cabinets that have drawers.

Before mortising hinges on an angle, I'd recommend practicing on some scraps until you feel confident enough to start digging into a finished cabinet.

Set back door from front

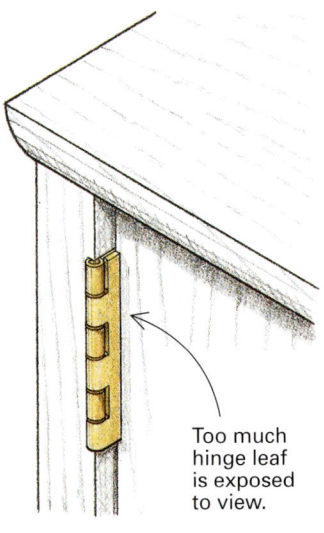

Too much hinge leaf is exposed to view.

Recess door from front

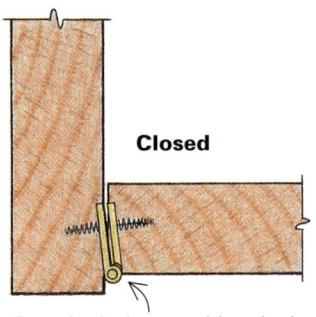

Closed

Door looks better with only the knuckle of the hinge showing.

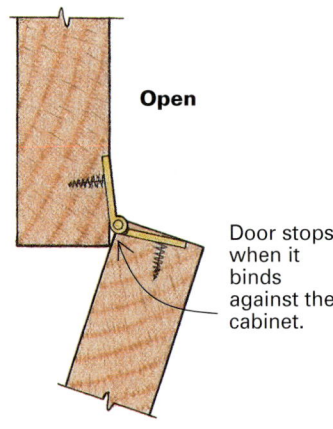

Open

Door stops when it binds against the cabinet.

Beaded stiles match the knuckles

Several years ago, when I first came to the Edward Barnsley workshop in Hampshire, England, for a six-month study program, I learned another unusual technique for installing butt hinges. It's one that I particularly like.

Just as with the method described above, the leaves are cut in at an angle, but the door fits flush with the front face of the cabinet (see the top drawing below). What makes this method unique is that you scratch a bead into the door stiles at precisely the same diameter as the knuckle of the hinge. So when the hinge is installed, it seems to melt into the cabinet.

This is a lovely detail, but just like the technique above, the door will bind when it's opened a little more than 90°. This method is especially well-suited for use in a corner cabinet like the one shown in the photo below.

Bury a hinge in a bead

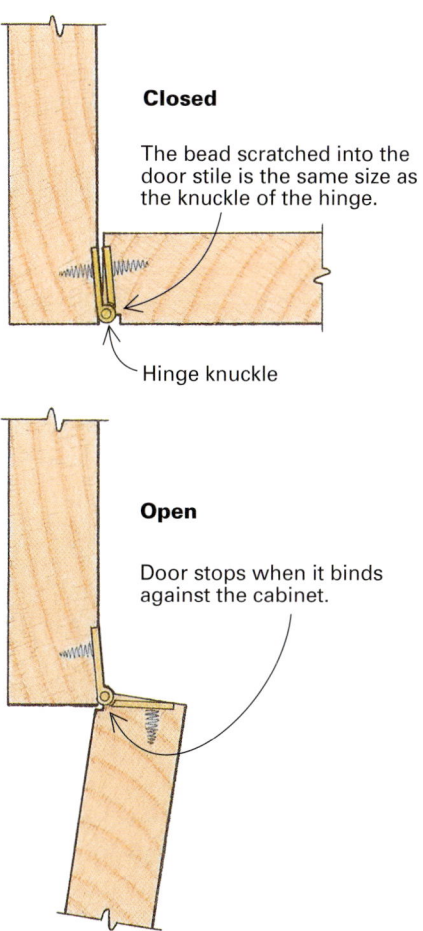

Closed

The bead scratched into the door stile is the same size as the knuckle of the hinge.

Hinge knuckle

Open

Door stops when it binds against the cabinet.

INSTALLING A HALF-MORTISE LOCK

by Philip C. Lowe

As a younger man, I served a stint in the Navy. I spent much of the time aboard the repair ship USS Jason out of San Diego, where I worked in the same shop alongside an older German patternmaker. I learned from him the importance of details. Not until some years later, after I'd set up shop as a furnituremaker, did I learn something (the hard way) about the value of details. I told a client who had commissioned a chest of drawers that I would throw in four locks with escutcheons for the cost of materials only. I figured the extra hardware would add just a few hours of labor to the project, and I could handle that.

Well into the eighth hour of installing the locks, I learned my lesson. When your livelihood depends on what you can accomplish in a given work day, time really is money. Now, when clients want an estimate on any job with doors or drawers, I always ask if they expect locks and escutcheons. They're usually amazed that such simple hardware can add so much to the total, but when they see a finished piece, they understand why.

What matters most is the kind and quality of lock you choose. If economy of time and material is important to you, a simple cylinder lock can be installed by drilling one hole and securing the lock with two screws. Surface locks are even easier because they are quickly attached with screws, no mortising.

I often use half-mortise locks. They're more expensive, but they really dress up a piece of furniture. They are set into the back surface of doors or drawers and flush to the edge. First-rate hardware for half-mortise locks is available from a number of suppliers.

Before you pick up your tools

The size and kind of lock you use on a piece of furniture will affect basic design decisions. When I build a cupboard door with a lock, I like the keyhole to fall dead center on the width of the visible stile—not the actual width, which might also include a rabbet for overlapping doors or a piece of applied molding. So I refer to hardware catalogs and check the critical dimensions: the width of the lip, the selvage, and the length and width of the back plate (see the drawing on the facing page). For a selvage dimension of $1\frac{1}{4}$ in., I would make my cupboard-door stile $2\frac{1}{2}$ in. wide.

I also determine whether the door (and required lock) are right- or left-handed. This specification can be very confusing, especially because not all manufacturers and dealers follow the same guidelines. But to make it simple, if you're standing in front of a cabinet with two doors (both hinged on the outside), the one on the left gets a right-hand lock. Be sure to check with your supplier on this detail. With drawer locks, the keyholes run perpendicular to the lip, so they are nonhanded. Some locks have the keyhole cut both horizontally and vertically, so they can be used with either a door or a drawer.

Half-mortise lock

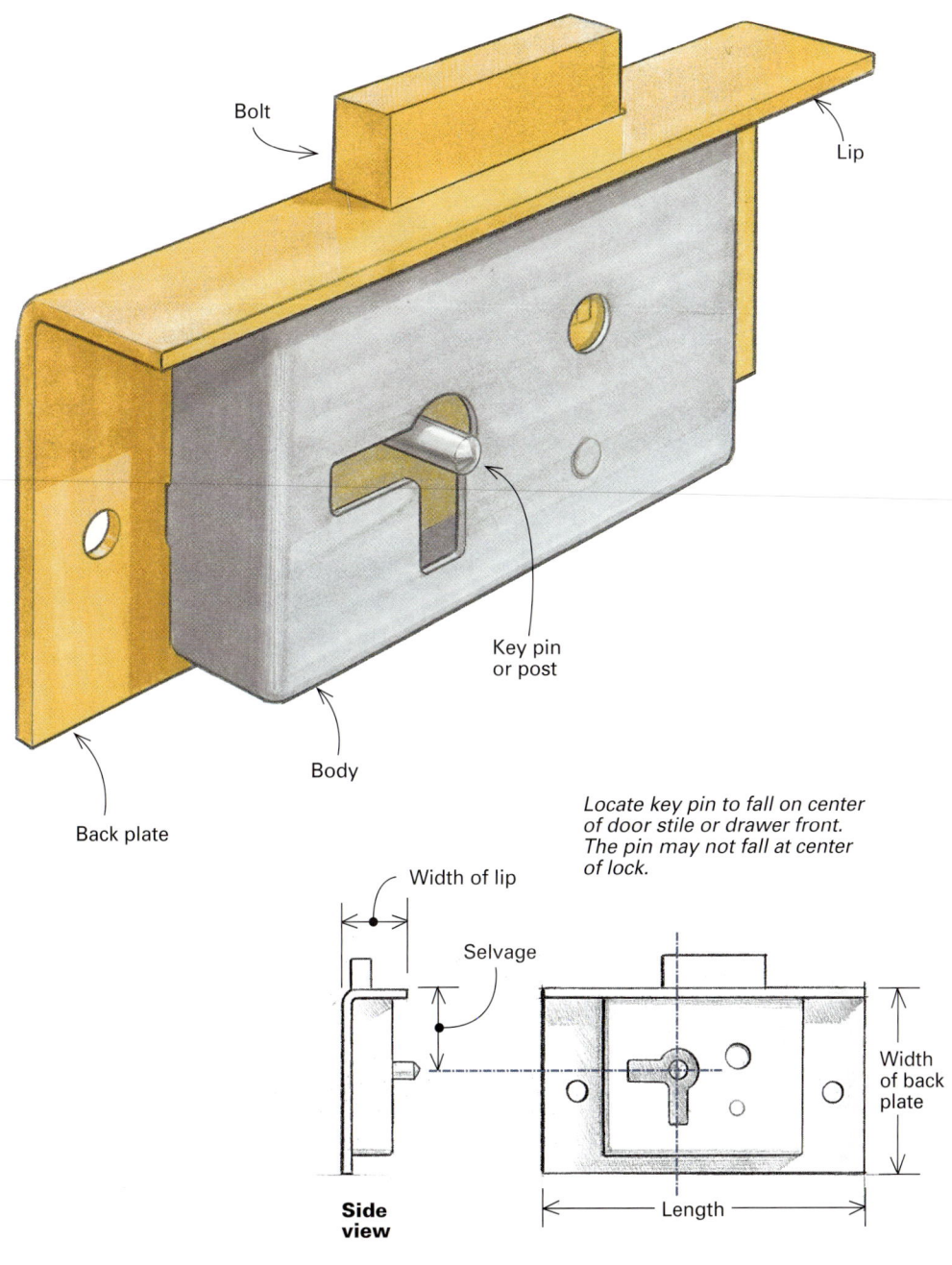

Bolt

Lip

Key pin
or post

Body

Back plate

Locate key pin to fall on center
of door stile or drawer front.
The pin may not fall at center
of lock.

Width of lip

Selvage

Width
of back
plate

**Side
view**

Length

Find the center

1. Set the marking gauge to the selvage first. All other layout dimensions flow from here.

2. Mark the center point for the key-pin hole, where the selvage meets the centerline of the workpiece.

3. Drill a small hole through the center point, using a bit just a little larger than the key-pin diameter. This hole will have to be enlarged later, depending on the type of escutcheon you choose.

4. Lay out mortise for the body. The lock is not on center, but the key pin is. Designs vary, so be sure to check this detail when you lay out your lock.

Mortise the body

5. Saw to the line to define the boundaries of the body mortise and to make chiseling easier. Some people might prefer to use a Japanese dozuki saw to make these cuts.

6. Relieve the inside edges of the mortise to prevent splitting and tear-out as material is removed. (The author made this chisel from an old jointer blade, a scrap of apple wood and a piece of copper pipe for the ferrule.)

Installing a half-mortise lock

I'm ready to install and fit a half-mortise lock once a door has been hinged or a drawer carcase has been assembled. With a small drawer, you might want to do the mortising before assembly for easier access to the drawer front.

Find the center, and fit the body first

You always should start by drawing a centerline on the outside face of the drawer front, extending the line across the top edge. Set a marking gauge to the selvage, the dis-

tance between the top of the lip to the center of the pin, and etch a short line where the selvage intersects the centerline (see photo 2). Drill a hole slightly larger than the diameter of the pin. Place the lock against the back of the drawer front, aligning the pin with the hole. Then draw two pencil lines on the top edge to indicate the width of the body (see photo 4). Using a square, transfer these lines to the back surface of the drawer front.

Set the marking gauge to the height of the body. Allow a little extra room if the bolt protrudes through the bottom of the lock body in the unlocked position. Some do, some don't. This little detail varies with the size of the lock and with the manufacturer. Scribe the back surface (parallel to the top edge), starting and stopping at your pencil lines. Then set the marking gauge to the thickness of the body, and transfer that line along the top edge.

With a backsaw, make two angled relief cuts along your pencil lines, stopping at the corners on the back and the top edge (see photo 5 on p. 113). Chisel away, flat side against the lines, removing waste as you go deeper into the mortise. I find that this method works better if I dig out a little at a time, chopping firmly against the grain and then cutting out the waste as I work down to the finished depth.

Follow with the lip mortise

Position the lock in the body mortise, and using a layout knife, score the lines on the top edge for the lip cutout. Set the marking

Mortising the lip and back plate

7. Set marking gauge for the thickness of the lip, and mark the inside face of the drawer front. Then place the lock into the body mortise, and scribe lines in the top edge with a layout knife.

8. Chisel to the lines made by marking gauge and layout knife. These shallow mortises require a deft and patient touch.

9. Once the lock body fits, score the back plate with a layout knife. This creates an incision into which you place the chisel edge for the final cut.Once the lock body fits, score the back plate with a layout knife. This creates an incision into which you place the chisel edge for the final cut.

10. Mortising for the back plate is fairly easy. The author is paring away most of one side in a single, clean stroke.

Fitting the escutcheon

11

14

12

15

13

11. Cast keyhole escutcheons taper front to back. Use the back, or smaller profile, to mark the door or drawer front.

12. Enlarge the piloted key-pin hole. Assemble the coping-saw blade through the hole, and make two straight cuts, following your traced lines.

13. Score the back; whack the front. With the correct-sized chisel, remaining waste usually comes out with little trouble.

14. Force-fit the escutcheon with a clamp. Cast pieces often are rough and may need to be cleaned up with a file first.

15. File and sand the good face flush. Start with 120-grit sandpaper, and work up to 400-grit silicone carbide to smooth the face and polish the brass.

Finishing Up

16. Dry-fit the lock, and screw it in place before marking and cutting the mortise for the bolt. The lock should be removed before any stain or finish is applied.

17. Check the key in the lock. The bolt should turn with a smooth, firm twist of the key.

16

17

gauge for the thickness of the lip, and transfer that mark along the back surface (see photo 7 on p. 114). Chisel the mortise for the lip, using feather cuts against the grain. Go easy, this is a delicate procedure. The lip sits just flush into the top edge of the drawer.

Fitting the back plate
Place the lock into position once again, and score the back-plate outline with the knife (see photo 9 on p. 114). Follow those lines with solid chisel chops. Using the marking gauge at the previous setting (lip and back plate should be the same thickness), scribe a line along the top inside edge of the drawer, within the mortise already cut for the lip. This represents the thickness of the back plate. Removing this waste should go smoothly if you use a sharp chisel. You're paring away only a small amount of material and pushing the chisel against the grain (see photo 10 on p. 114).

Cutting the keyhole
Determine the size hole needed for the key, which will depend on your choice for the escutcheon (see the box on the facing page). Drill it. Scribe the shape of the keyhole with a pencil, and cut the keyhole, using a coping saw with the blade assembled through the

hole. With a small, sharp chisel, the waste usually will pop right out in one clean strike. If not, you can fine-tune the hole with small files and rasps. I used a keyhole rim for the job shown in photos 11-15 on the facing page. If you choose an inlaid escutcheon made of a brittle material, it's a good idea to start your hole with a countersink first and follow with a drill bit. That will prevent the cutting spur of the bit from damaging the surrounding surface. After you've cut the keyhole and fitted the escutcheon, you can dry-fit the lock in place. Bore pilot holes for the screws, and secure the lock (see photo 16).

Mortising for the bolt
Now it's time to make a mortise cut in the cabinet for the bolt. Place the drawer in its opening, slightly ajar. Turn the key so the bolt is in the locked position. Gently push the drawer in place until the bolt rests against the drawer divider, and mark those lines. Using a small square, transfer the lines to the underside of the divider. Determine the distance of the bolt from the front of the drawer, accounting for any reveals when the drawer rests against its stops. Mark those lines, and chop out a mortise slightly over-sized—a little play won't hurt.

Choosing an escutcheon

This antique silver escutcheon is set into a bird's-eye box.

Escutcheons, the decorative plates that surround keyholes, can be purchased in a range of styles (see the photo below). You can buy everything from flat, circular or geometric shapes to cast ornamental forms with a high-relief detail and gilded ones known as ormolu.

There are three basic types of escutcheons: those mounted to the surface, inlaid designs cut to shape and set into the surface, and cast rims in keyhole shapes, which are set into the opening of the hole.

When selecting an escutcheon, be sure it will fit well. Refer to the dimensions in the catalog when you're in the design stage, and make the door stile or drawer front the right size for the selvage and the lip.

If possible, buy the hardware before you begin building.

Surface-mounted escutcheons come in styles to match those from William and Mary designs (early 18th century) through Arts and Crafts (early 20th century) to contemporary versions. You don't like any of those styles? Make your own, or carve a shape in wax and have it cast. Keep in mind this approach will add a lot of time (and cost) to the project.

Inlaid escutcheons offer more flexibility if you want to make your own to any shape or size. You can make inlaid escutcheons out of just about anything—wood, brass, silver, nickel, gold, pewter, mother-of-pearl, ivory or stone. These can be set into the surface before the keyhole is drilled.

Keyhole rims come as rough castings, slightly tapered from front to back.

On first-rate work, I usually spend some time cleaning them with fine files, inside and out, taking care not to file away the taper. When set into the surface, they are a press fit, so the layout on the door or drawer face is done using the narrow end.

Surface-mounted plates are affixed to the surface with escutcheon pins (brass nails) or brass screws. Or the plates are secured from behind with screws into threaded posts. Inlaid plates can be glued in place. Epoxy works well for metal, stone and ivory; for other materials, your standard wood glue should work just fine.

Factory-made escutcheons—Styles can match drop pull hardware (left) and many smaller surface-mounted versions (center). Inlaid versions (right) require more work to install.

If you're working within a limited space (a shallow drawer), use a chisel pitched at a steep cutting angle, so the bevel is perpendicular to the divider. On the finest work, you often will find a strike plate set flush into the divider for extra protection from the prying hands of over-zealous children or adults with criminal intent.

A good-quality mortise lock with an escutcheon can make all the difference in the finished look of a piece of furniture. Keith, a former student of mine at the North Bennet Street School in Boston, would say that it was "slicker than deer guts on a doorknob." In case that leaves you wondering, he meant it as a compliment.

SIX

Molding

Moldings are those additions or variations on furniture that add life and interest. They are seldom structurally necessary, though often serve an important purpose. Some styles of furniture are almost defined by their absence, such as Shaker, while other styles are almost defined by them, such as the Victorian styles. A spare Victorian bookcase, one without an overwhelming number of moldings, is almost a contradiction in terms. Used conservatively, though, a molding or molded edge can transform a piece of furniture from dull and dowdy to subtly interesting and, frankly, beautiful.

To make moldings, there are basically three choices: buying them ready-made, making them with a router or a shaper, or making them with hand tools. Bought moldings eliminate a lot of shop work, but of course limit your choices to whatever is manufactured. The most commonly available moldings are for architectural trim. They're often too large for small-scale furniture making and are made in paint-grade woods. Still, there are sources for furniture moldings that make this option viable.

The most common use for a router is to mold edges and make moldings. Think of the hundreds of furniture molding-profile bits available in any hardware store. It's hard to go wrong with this route. Routers are very efficient and produce crisp profiles. Handmade molding techniques are always good to know when a router won't do or when you're aiming for a traditional look. Scratch stocks, beaders, molding, and combination planes all do excellent work on a small scale. Perhaps the greatest advantage is that you can make cutters to the exact profile you want—you're not limited to available molding or router bits.

Integrating moldings into the piece is another matter. Moldings often need to run across the grain. If wood movement isn't taken into consideration, "pop" goes the molding. Many antiques in otherwise good shape suffer from lost or broken moldings for just this reason. Chris Becksvoort has a traditional solution to this that will last for generations.

SIMPLE TOOLS CAN REPRODUCE MOST MOLDINGS

by Robert S. Judd

Scratch stocks—old, new and shopmade—Whether old like the Stanley #66 (right), new like the Lie-Nielsen #66 reproduction (left) or shopmade (top), these scratch stocks are a simple way to reproduce moldings or create new designs accurately and economically.

Scratch stocks function beautifully, quickly and economically to duplicate handworked wood trim. By simply grinding or filing a cutter to the appropriate profile, you can reproduce almost any shape molding up to about 1 in. wide. Scratch stocks, or beading tools as they are sometimes called, are readily available new (Lie-Nielsen Toolworks, Inc., Route 1, Warren, Maine 04864; 800-327-2520 or Veritas Tools Inc., 12 East River St., Ogdensburg, N.Y. 13669; 800-667-2986), used (antique tool dealers, garage sales or flea markets) or shopmade (see the photo on the facing page). I make mine from a 6-in.-long, L-shaped piece of stock. The cutter fits into a sawkerf, and it is clamped in place with a few screws, as shown in the photo on the facing page. The cutters for all of these tools are easily shaped from old scrapers and sawblades or new blanks from Lie-Nielsen or Veritas.

In my repair and restoration business, I often need to duplicate broken or missing moldings. Usually, only a foot or two of the molding is needed: hardly worth the effort of setting up the router and definitely not worth having a cutter ground to match one of the myriad of molding shapes. Besides, no power tool can match the irregularities of the handworked wood found in older pieces.

Scratch stocks and beaders

First made by users as a simple holder for a scraper blade, scratch stocks included a fence arrangement to work a measured distance from an edge. The beading tool was essentially an improved, factory-made scratch stock and included a range of cutters in different sizes and several blanks, custom-filed to fit the user's needs. Adjustable fences for both straight and curved edges were often included. A scratch stock or beader can produce a carbon copy of the original molding by using a cutter that's simply filed to shape.

Shaping the cutter

To make a basic beaded molding, take a sample piece of beading, a file and a blade blank and set to work filing a negative pattern of the molding, as shown in the top left photo. As you file the pattern into the blade, keep testing its fit (see the bottom photo on p. 122). Check the fit frequently because it is fairly easy to file past the desired shape. It's a good idea to leave a $1/8$-in.-wide metal strip at either edge of the cutter. Narrower strips tend to bend and lose their effectiveness. Old cabinet scrapers or sawblade sections make good cutters for shopmade scratch stocks. But for my 100-year-old Stanley #66 hand beader, the blanks that

Beading is simple with a scratch stock—Just hold the fence against the stock and make repeated passes, about ¹⁄₁₆ in. per pass, until the appropriate depth has been reached.

Matching a molding to a cutter is crucial to reproducing old moldings. File the cutter to the negative image of the molding. Check the cutter frequently while filing to make sure it is an accurate match.

Lie-Nielsen makes for his gem-like bronze replicas of the #66 work well. The steel of the new blanks is not hardened, so the blanks are easy to file to shape. After filing them to shape, hone just the cutter's faces in a whetstone to provide a clean cutting edge. I've never found it necessary to harden a cutter once it's filed to shape.

Making moldings

When producing short moldings, I've found it easier to work the edge of my board, as shown in the bottom left photo. For making small beads or moldings, I cut two lengths at once by working both corners of the same board edge. Begin the scraping process by firmly gripping the handles, and push or pull the tool across the board's edge, keeping the handles at 90° to the work. Take small

scrapings initially, only ¹⁄₁₆ in. or so at a time. Because stock removal is done by scraping, a small cut gives much more control and does less damage if you slip. As the cutter starts to bottom out, you can continuously adjust the blade so more is exposed. In a surprisingly short time, the molding will start to appear on the edge. If the cutter starts to chatter or jump, you are probably trying to remove too much material, or the grain might be changing; use a little less pressure, or try changing the direction of cut.

One of the handy features of the #66 or the Lie-Nielsen reproduction is the adjustable fence. When cutting two lengths of molding on a board edge, the fence can be set to cut the opposite corner without moving the blade. This lets you produce a surprising amount of molding in a relatively short time. I make several extra moldings, so I can pick the best match to the original.

I like to start the staining and coloring process at this stage because the strips are far easier to handle while they are still attached to a board. Often, I will even do the preliminary finishing and filling at this point for the same reason. It's then a simple matter to trim the finished molding off on the tablesaw. I set the saw fence to leave a little extra material, which I later trim off with a utility knife.

When repairing antique pieces, mark your name and date on the back of the new molding for historical reference. After all, with a matching stain and finish, the repair should be almost invisible.

Other applications

In addition to producing molding patterns, this highly functional family of tools is also effective for routing and inlay work. Because you create the cutters to fit the situation at hand, you are no longer limited to standard router bits.

When using these tools to rout cross-grain, however, it's a good idea to lay out the material to be removed by lightly cutting in the lines with a sharp craft knife. The scored lines help prevent tearout, which could ruin your project.

MOLDING THAT STAYS PUT

by Christian Becksvoort

Ask any antique collector or dealer about the most common problem with old case pieces and you're sure to hear a familiar refrain: The molding's always the first thing to go. Attaching molding to a solid carcase side is a problem. A wide case piece, such as a chest of drawers, can move $3/8$ in. to $1/2$ in. through the seasons as the ambient humidity rises and falls. Molding glued or nailed to the case sides, its grain perpendicular to the grain of the sides, isn't moving at all. There are two possible outcomes.

Either the case sides will crack because the molding has prevented them from moving, or the molding will fall off because the side has moved and broken the glue bond between case side and molding.

I get around these problems by attaching side molding with a series of dovetailed keys (see the photo on p. 124 and the photo and drawing on p. 125). A dovetailed slot cut in the back of the side molding allows it to slide onto the short dovetailed keys attached to the case. The connection keeps the molding snugged up tight to the carcase. But because the molding is not glued to the carcase or to the keys, the case sides are free to move. This technique has been used for centuries and is still found on the highest caliber work. It takes a little extra effort to attach molding this way, but the molding will last as long as the case piece, and the case sides will not crack.

Preparing the carcase and the molding

The case sides must be perfectly flat all the way across if the molding is to fit correctly. To check for flatness, I set the case on one side and hold a straightedge across the top

edge of the exposed side. I pencil mark any high spots and beltsand the side flat. Then I flip the case over and repeat the process on the other side.

Once the case sides are flat, the front molding can be attached to the case. I miter one end of the front molding, position it in

This molding will last as long as the chest. Applied over dovetailed keys, the molding will allow the case sides to move seasonally.

place and mark the other end. After cutting the second miter, I glue the molding to the front of the case. The grain direction of the molding is the same as the case, so wood movement isn't a problem.

Routing the dovetailed slot in two passes
I rout the dovetailed slot in the two pieces of side molding in two passes on my router table. I remove the bulk of the slot with a straight bit. For the second pass, I use a 1/2-in.-wide dovetail bit set to full-depth, about 1/4 in. for the 1 1/8-in.-high molding I used on this chest (see the top photo at left on p. 126). On smaller case pieces, I use a molding that's 7/8 in. high and rout a 3/8-in.-wide slot, also 1/4 in. deep. For either size molding, I position the dovetailed slot just a

little bit higher than the center of the molding, so it's not weakened excessively.

When I have finished routing slots in both side pieces (and in some extra stock, just in case), I check the depth with a dial caliper. This depth reading gives me the precise thickness for the dovetailed keys. Be sure to check it in several places along each piece of molding. The depth can vary slightly if pressure on the moldings isn't absolutely consistent when routing the slots. I generally don't find variations of more than 0.005 in., which is not a problem. I just thickness the keys to the shallowest reading taken with the dial caliper (see the bottom photo at left on p. 126). If there's more variation than 0.005 in. overall, I'll re-rout new molding.

Making the dovetailed keys

I make the keys from a blank that's a little thicker than 1/2 in., about 3 in. wide and a few inches longer than the case sides. Before cutting the keys for the case, I use a piece of scrap of the same thickness to make a test piece, adjusting the fence on the router table until the fit is snug but non-binding. I rout a dovetailed profile onto both sides of the blank, top and bottom (see the top right photo on p. 126). Then I saw off the keys with a little to spare.

Keys are taken to final thickness in a planer. Because the keys are so thin, I use an auxiliary bed to prevent snipe. I take material off the narrower side of the keys, checking the thickness with a dial caliper after each pass (see the bottom left photo on p. 126). The keys should be between 0.003 in. and 0.005 in. thinner than the slot depth, so the molding will be pulled tightly to the case.

Attaching the keys as continuous strips

A series of keys, not one long piece, holds each side molding to the case sides. But if installed as separate keys, alignment could be a real headache. Instead, I attach the keys as one continuous strip on each side of the case and then chop out the waste between individual keys, which are glued and screwed to the case. This allows the case

sides to move and ensures that all the keys are in line, making it much easier to slide the molding home.

The first step in attaching the keys is positioning them. I hold a strip of molding against the side of the case, with the top edge of the molding flush with or just slightly proud of the top of the case (it's easier to remove a little bit of molding than it is to level the whole top down to the mold-

Attaching moldings with dovetailed keys _____

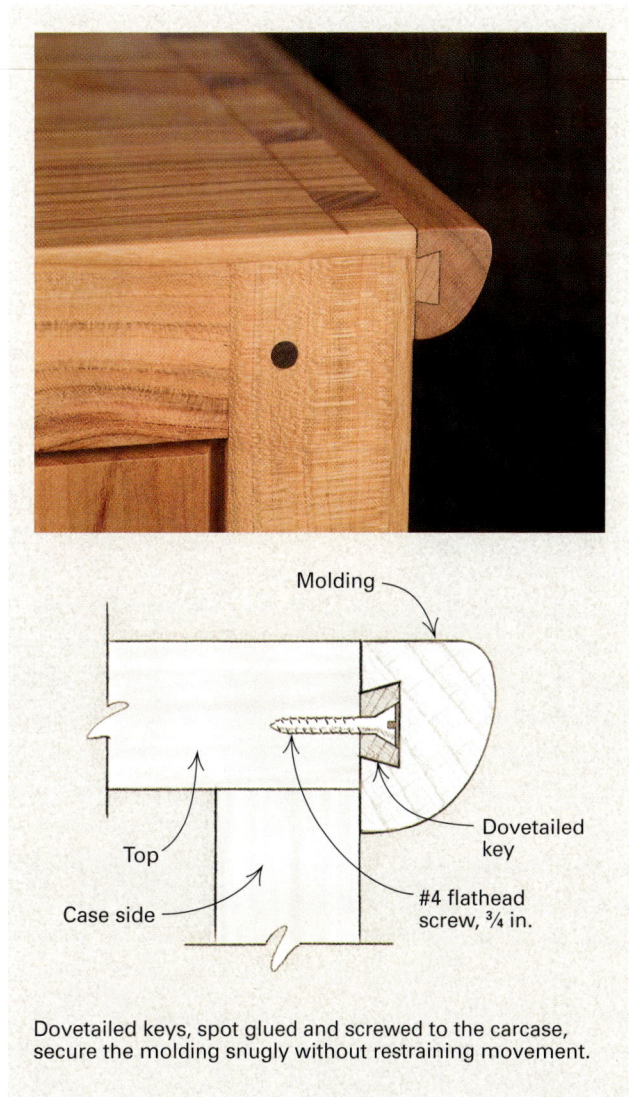

Dovetailed keys, spot glued and screwed to the carcase, secure the molding snugly without restraining movement.

Labels: Molding, Dovetailed key, Top, Case side, #4 flathead screw, 3/4 in.

Rout the dovetailed slot in two passes.
Start the slot in the molding with a straight bit; then make a second pass with a dovetail bit set to full depth.

Rout the dovetailed keys. Use a piece of scrap to set the fence on the router table, making adjustments until the key fits snugly into the molding slot.

Plane the keys to thickness. Check with a dial caliper after each pass. Keys should be 0.003 in. to 0.005 in. thinner than the slot is deep.

Tack keys in place. A dab of glue and a brad at the center of each key hold the strip in place.

ing). With a knife, I mark both the top and bottom of the dovetailed slot, at the front and rear of the case. Then I connect these marks using a straightedge. I now have the position of my key strip.

The next step is to lay out where the keys will be and where waste will be removed between them after the key strip has been attached. Because I've built quite a few of these five-drawer chests, I have a pattern. I made the pattern by marking out the center of the key strip, and then dividing each half into three keys separated by ¹/₂-in. spaces. I marked for screws about ¹/₂ in. to either side of the centers of the individual keys.

I put a dab of glue at the center of each of the marked keys and then tack the strip with some ³/₄-in., #20 brads (see the bottom right photo on the facing page). I countersink holes for the screws that ultimately hold the keys in place and drive home the 3/4-in., #4 screws by hand (see the photo at right). The waste between the keys is chopped out with a chisel and a mallet (see the photo at right below).

Easing assembly

I take just a sliver off the leading edge of each key and the dovetailed slot in the molding, so the molding will slide home more easily. Then I lubricate the inside of the dovetailed slot with a bit of graphite by rubbing the sides and bottom of the slot with a no. 2 pencil. Keep it back at least 2 in. from the miter, where the molding will be glued.

I test the fit of the molding, sanding the tops of the keys slightly if they seem too tight. The molding should slide right onto the keys without binding. After testing the fit, I put a dab of glue on the miter and on the first 2 in. of the case and then tap the molding home. I clamp the molding across the case at the miter. After the glue has dried, I saw off the excess at the back of the case.

Countersink holes, and then screw the keys down. A little beeswax applied to the screw threads will make the job easier and reduce the chance of a screw breaking.

Chop out the waste. The author uses a mallet and a sharp chisel to remove waste between keys. Any chisel marks between keys will be hidden by the molding.

DRESSING UP A BASIC BOX

by Phil Lowe

Easily applied elements can dramatically alter a cabinet's appearance. I added clustered columns, an octagonal base, waist moldings and a blocked cornice along with a quatrefoil and arched surround to a simple frame-and-panel base cabinet and an open bookshelf top unit. The result was Gothic detailing that would blend into my client's home. These elements also create a dramatic play of light and shadow, particularly in a piece to be painted. And, ironically, the most complicated detail I added, the intricately carved cornice block, is the easiest to use. It is a precast piece that simply glues in place (see the story on p. 132).

Building the cabinets

The basic forms started with two rectangular boxes, as shown in the drawing on p. 131. The tops and bottoms, arched surround and backs were made up of ³/₄-in.-thick, lumber-core birch plywood. The sides and doors were poplar frames with ¹/₄-in.-thick birch plywood panels. Ogee moldings glued and nailed around the inside edges of the door and side frames add more detailing and shadow lines. Before assembling the boxes, holes were drilled into the stiles of the case sides for adjustable shelving pins. The cases were glued and screwed together with the screws located so the cornice, base and waist moldings would cover the screw heads.

Add-on moldings create a new look—
Tacking on some simple moldings has transformed a basic pair of boxes into a Gothic showpiece. One key to the fine detailing is the precast composition capital, which saved hours of carving time.

Adding a Gothic arch

To make the Gothic arch, the lumber-core birch plywood was cut to width and length. Plywood eliminated panel glue up and minimized any expansion or shrinkage that would play havoc with the cornice and arched moldings. After the arch was laid out and bandsawn to shape, it was rabbeted to receive the molding that covers the plywood's edge. The molding for the arch (see the drawing detail on p. 131) was shaped with an ogee curve on the front face, a quarter round with fillet on the opposite edge and a rabbet on the back to mate with the rabbet on the plywood. The curved section of this molding was faceplate-turned on the lathe. These moldings were cut to size, glued and nailed to the arch. The arch was glued and screwed in place.

Joining top to bottom

Before assembling the two cases, filler pieces were applied around the bottom of the upper case, as shown in the drawing. These filler pieces help position the top and provide screw blocks for securing the top to the bottom. The top case was then positioned

Molding hides joinery details—The waist molding provides a smooth transition from upper to lower case, and it hides the joint where the two units meet.

Details make the difference—The pointed-arch panel dressed up with detailing sets off the upper bookcase unit. The author purchased the elaborate molded capitals and only had to glue them in place.

on the lower case and the cases temporarily screwed together. The cases can be separated for moving, but I wanted the top and bottom units screwed together when applying the waist molding that hides the joint between the two units.

Applying base moldings

To provide a platform for the clustered columns, two half-octagonal blocks were glued to the face of the base cabinet, as shown in the drawing. Two different base moldings were mitered to wrap around the corners and the octagonal blocks and then glued and nailed in position.

Defining the waist

The waist molding was composed of a lower cove, central torus and an upper ogee and hides the joint between the two cases. The torus is glued and nailed flush with the bottom edge of the top case after applying the half-octagonal blocks, as shown in the drawing. The cove molding, butted tight to the bottom edge of the torus, provides a smooth transition into the lower case. After applying the half-octagonal blocks, the cove was glued and nailed to the top edge of the lower case. The ogee, the width of which was determined by the distance from the top of the torus to the top of the bottom shelf, was glued and nailed. Make sure that the bottom edge is seated against the top of the torus. It is better to make this molding a hair wider than needed than to make it too narrow. The molding can be trimmed easily to the shelf, but it wouldn't take much to sand through the thin veneer face of the birch plywood while leveling the shelf to the molding.

The cornice tops it off

The cornice at the top of the upper bookshelves went on in three stages: the ogee (or cyma recta) first, the reverse ogee (or cyma reversa) second and the fillet last. These moldings wrap around a rectangular cornice block at the top of the clustered column.

The size of the block was determined by the precast capitals that I bought (see the story on p. 132).

Capitals and columns

Once the cornice has been applied, the capitals are pushed tight to the underside of the cornice blocks and glued and screwed to the case from the inside. The two-piece clustered columns were fabricated by molding the two edges on the inner piece slightly more than quarter round. The outer portion of the column was molded to a shape a bit more than half-round in section (see the drawing detail on the facing page). These shapes were glued and nailed together to form the clustered columns and then cut to length to fit between the octagonal blocks and capitals on the upper case. Cluster columns also were cut to length and glued in place between the half-octagonal blocks of the base cabinet.

Applied decorations

The quatrefoils and panels that reflect the shape of the space above the arch are also applied pieces. Their layout was done by drawing concentric curves and parallel lines to the arch, cornice and clustered columns. Three circles were drawn to create spaces around the quatrefoils and space in the center. The quatrefoils were drawn inside a circle concentric to the first circle. Once molded and sanded, the decorations were glued and nailed in place.

Decorating the doors

The doors were constructed with a solid frame, plywood panel and ogee molding. The outer edges of the door frames were decorated with the same shaped molding used along the inner edge of the Gothic arch. This molding created a thicker door. When mounting the hinges, the fillet of the molding was aligned with the front surface of the cabinet, and the hinge knuckle was fully exposed for more swing.

Gothic bookcase

*Simple moldings added to a pair of plain boxes
transform them into an elaborate Gothic showpiece.*

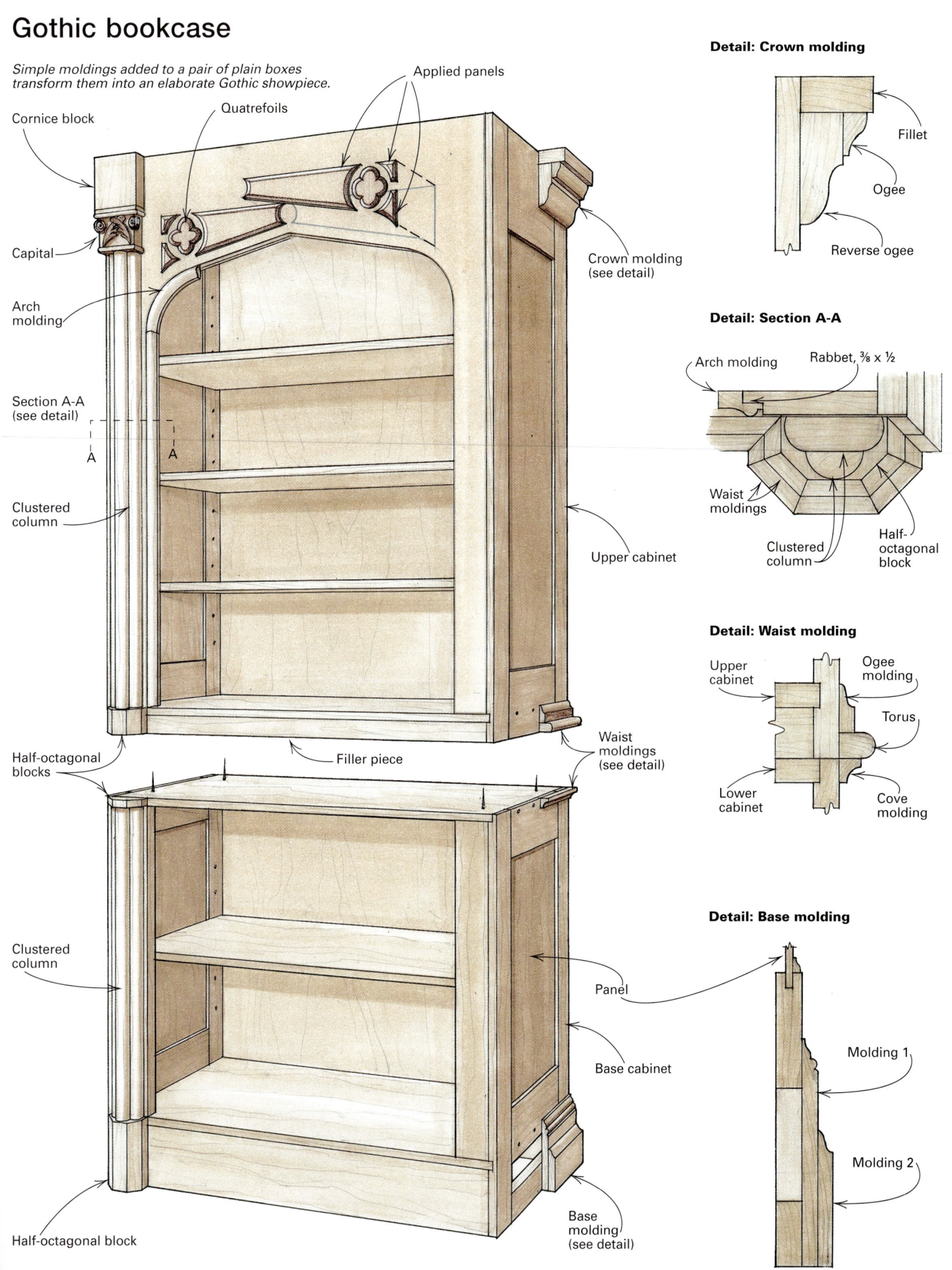

Cornice block

Quatrefoils

Applied panels

Capital

Arch
molding

Section A-A
(see detail)

Clustered
column

Crown molding
(see detail)

Upper cabinet

Half-octagonal
blocks

Filler piece

Waist
moldings
(see detail)

Clustered
column

Panel

Base cabinet

Half-octagonal block

Base
molding
(see detail)

Detail: Crown molding

Fillet

Ogee

Reverse ogee

Detail: Section A-A

Arch molding

Rabbet, ⅜ × ½

Waist
moldings

Clustered
column

Half-
octagonal
block

Detail: Waist molding

Upper
cabinet

Ogee
molding

Torus

Lower
cabinet

Cove
molding

Detail: Base molding

Molding 1

Molding 2

Precast ornaments save time, effort and money

Precast ornaments, or compo decorations, are molded from wood fibers or resins and binders, usually hide glue. This material can be molded accurately to duplicate intricately carved details (see the photo). Precast ornaments can be stained, and on painted pieces, they can fool experienced woodworkers. They cost from a few dollars up to several hundred dollars, but they can save laborious hours of carving, especially on painted furniture.

Selecting precast ornaments

Although precast ornaments can be custom-made, there's a vast array of stock designs. To get the most out of stock ornaments, however, it's best to select ornaments during the planning phase, so you can alter the design to fit available sizes. All the suppliers offer catalogs, and some of these catalogs offer extensive application, design information and product listings. If you're going to use compo moldings regularly, the catalogs are quite helpful.

Durability and working characteristics

Precast ornaments are fairly durable and somewhat pliable when fresh. After application or with age, they harden to an almost china consistency but not as fragile. The manufacturers recommend not ordering too far in advance, so they'll be fresh and more easily manipulated.

Because the ornaments are made with hide glue, a separate adhesive is not required. The glue is reconstituted by steam, softening the ornament and making it more pliable. When steamed a bit longer than usual, they can be molded into concave shapes or around convex curves by pressing them in place with your fingers. The decorations can be applied to wood, plaster, drywall, metal or mirrors.

Applying the ornaments

No special surface treatment is required, but surfaces should be clean, dry, smooth and dust-free to ensure a good bond.

To steam the ornaments, you'll need a heat source, such as a double hot plate or camp stove, a tray large enough to hold the ornaments and a ¼-in.-sq. mesh screen with canvas stretched over it for setting the ornaments on, as shown in the photo. The pan or tray is filled with water and heated on the hot plates to a low, steady boil. The canvas covered screen is bent to support the ornaments about an inch above the water surface. Two or three ornaments at a time are set on the canvas, which should be coated with a thin layer of hide glue. The fresher an ornament is, the less steam time it will need: usually 30 seconds to two minutes. Aged ornaments will take longer. The ornament is ready when the bottom surface is slightly wet, sticky and the ornament is pliable.

When the ornament is ready, lift it from the canvas with a spatula, and place it where needed. You have a few moments to adjust and position it before it begins to harden and adhere. Be careful not to burn your fingers, and be sure to turn down the heat if you get too much steam. Once the ornament is in place, a chisel or knife can be used to clean the ornament if needed.

The canvas should be kept clean by dipping a brush into the steaming water and scrubbing the canvas. Oversteaming can cause the ornaments to become too soft or too wet. Oversteamed ornaments should be left to cool, design side down, or blotted on cardboard before applying. Cooled ornaments can be re-steamed, if necessary. If you place an ornament incorrectly, it can be removed with a spatula within 10 minutes of application, reheated and reapplied.

Applying precast moldings is easy, requiring no special equipment and can dramatically transform a case. And the moldings are inexpensive compared to hand-carving the intricate details.

MAKING OGEE BRACKET FEET

by Sam Fletcher

I made a stack of Chippendale-style mirrors for our annual church sale, and I was disappointed when they didn't sell as well as I'd hoped. When the next sale rolled around, I looked for a more successful project. I had read that small jewelry boxes are very popular at craft sales, so I decided to make them my next project for our fund-raiser.

Boxes are simple, and they are easily made, even in quantity. But they can be awfully plain. I wanted to dress them up a

Bracket feet give a box new stature. These feet can be made easily and in any size.

Plastic laminate

Dowel, ⅜ in.

Simplify bracket feet with a template. A scrap of plastic laminate makes a good template for laying out the decorative scroll on these feet. The dowel quickly and accurately locates the template in the blank.

A cove cut is the first step in developing the profile. The author makes a ⅜-in. cove on both edges of a piece of stock.

bit. I liked the effect that feet add to the overall look of a jewelry box. Small ogee bracket feet elevate a box both figuratively and literally (see the photo on p. 133).

High-volume shops use custom tooling to make ogee bracket feet, but my method uses a standard cove (or flute) cutter and basic hand and machine tools. Although I developed this method to make miniature feet, the general procedure can be used for making larger feet as well.

Make a template and glue jig first

Decorative scrolls on the wings of these miniature feet give them a distinctive Chippendale look. To speed the layout of this scroll, I made a template from plastic laminate and a small piece of ⅜-in. dowel (see the photos at left). The dowel registers the template in each foot blank, saving me the trouble of locating the profile each time. The template also makes the feet consistent.

It can be tricky to glue small mitered pieces, so the simple jigs I make from 2-in.-sq., 1-in.-thick oak pieces are a great help (see the bottom photo on p. 137). I bore a ¼-in. hole in the center of each square and cut a 90° angle out of one side. The hole permits the pieces to fit together properly and takes care of glue squeeze-out. I use a 3-in. spring clamp and a short length of ¼-in. dowel to hold the pieces together.

Making the ogee profile

I use a board 6 in. to 8 in. wide, surfaced to 1 in. thick, for a 1-in.-high foot. The stock thickness corresponds to the height of the foot. To make feet for a box like the ones shown in the photo on p. 133, I use a board about 2 ft. long.

Using a wider board is faster because I can work on two edges at once, ripping them as I go. Having the extra width also makes machining the wood less dangerous.

I start by making the S-shaped ogee profile in the edge of the stock. The ogee can be very dramatic or subtle depending on how deeply I cut the groove and the size of the radius on the top edge.

Round over the top edge. A block plane fairs a cove into the rounded edge at the top of the foot.

Rip the molding to width. The author cuts one edge, flips the stock around and rips the opposite edge.

With a shopmade cutoff stop, you don't have to mark each piece. Two miter gauges, set at 45° and 90°, also speed the work.

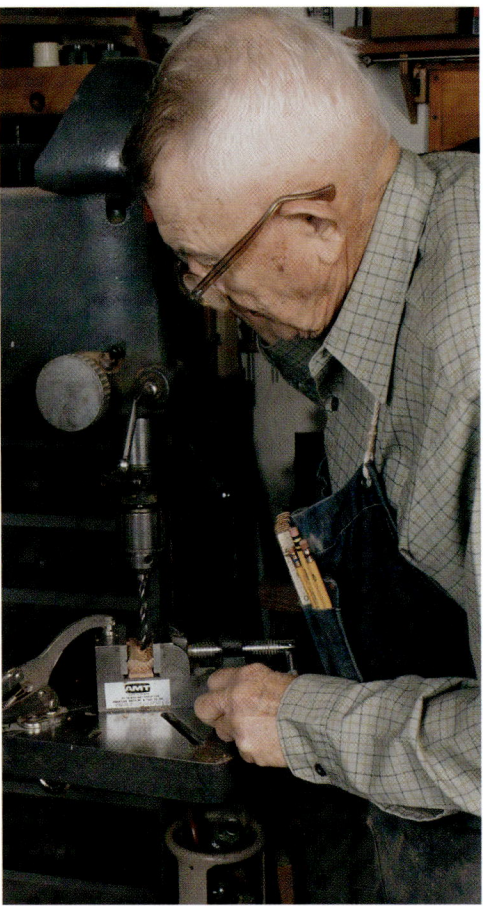

Bore the hole for the scroll profile. The hole is part of the profile and provides registration for the scroll template. A vise holds the workpiece precisely.

Mark out the scroll. The dowel locates the template on the pieces. The profile is laid out on the back of each foot piece.

I cut a groove for the concave part of the ogee curve on my shaper. For the 1-in.-high feet that I'm making here, I use a ³/₈-in. cove cutter set about ¹/₈ in. above the table to define the base of the foot. The fence is set so the cove is ¹/₄ in. deep. I cut the groove on both long edges of the stock (see the bottom photo on p. 134).

I complete the ogee by rounding over the convex portion of the profile with a small block plane (see the top photo on p. 135). Scrapers made from an old hacksaw blade allow me to make any final corrections in the shape before the pieces are sanded.

Ripping the stock to width and mitering

Now I rip a piece of molding from each edge of the stock (see the bottom left photo on p. 135). I set the rip fence to ⁵/₈ in., rip one side and then flip the board around and rip the other side.

The next step is to cut and miter the pieces to length. I bought my Sears tablesaw new in 1940 and have made a number of useful attachments for it. One of them is an adjustable cutoff stop that eliminates the need for marking each piece (see the bottom right photo on p. 135).

To really make cutting and mitering easier, I made additional miter gauges out of ³/₈-in. by ³/₄-in. steel flat bar and aluminum angle. I keep one of these miter gauges set at 90° and another one set at 45°.

With these two miter gauges, I don't need to stop and reset the angle. I miter-cut one end, flip the stock end for end and then miter-cut the other end. Then, using the 90°

miter gauge and the adjustable stop, I cut the piece to length, flip the stock end for end again, and cut the other piece to length. I repeat this process until I have cut enough pieces.

Lay out and cut the scroll

The scroll at the bottom edge of the foot starts with a ³⁄₈-in. hole bored in each piece. This hole forms part of the scroll profile, but more important, it is the reference for the scroll template. Therefore, the hole must be bored accurately. To do this, I use a machinist's vise on my drill-press table and a brad-point bit.

I separate the work into right- hand and left-hand pieces and then register one end of a piece flush with the edge of the vise jaw. To align the vise and workpiece under the bit, I place the template on the stock with the narrow end of the template flush with the square end of the workpiece.

The drill bit is lowered until it is just above the template. I position the vise so that the registration plug on the template is aligned with the bit and clamp the vise on the drill-press table. I remove the template, bore all the like-handed parts (see the photo at left on the facing page), reposition the vise and then bore the rest.

Using the scroll template, I mark out all the pieces, as shown in the center photo above. Because the face of each foot piece already has been profiled, the scroll is laid out on the back side. I use a jigsaw to cut out the scroll shape (see the photo at right above).

Glue jig speeds assembly

I group all the pieces into left-right assemblies, spread glue on the mitered surfaces and rub the pieces together. I clamp together the assemblies using the glue jig, dowel and spring clamp (see the photo at right). Once the glue has dried, I lightly sand the outside surface of each foot. I use a chainsaw file for smoothing the scroll. The feet are ready to be glued to the box.

Cut the scroll. The author uses a jigsaw to cut the scroll profile.

Clamp the parts. Gluing jigs hold the pieces at 90° and give glue squeeze-out a place to go. The dowel bridging the two pieces is temporary.

SEVEN

Veneering

Veneering is a term that casts fear into the hearts of many otherwise talented woodworkers. It ranks among steam-bending and green woodworking as one of the more mysterious, difficult-to-fathom techniques. When wood gets thin—down to tiny fractions of an inch—it ceases to behave like larger boards. Without a familiar frame of reference, woodworkers shy away from trying to work with it. But oh, the places you shall go if you do!

Traditional hide glue-and-hammer veneering techniques work perfectly well and are no more troublesome to learn than any other woodworking technique. But there are easier ways. Vacuum bags have taken veneering into the 21st century. But if you don't have the cash for such a system, there is a very cheap, excellent alternative: ironing dried yellow glue.

Michael Burton and Mario Rodriguez both use this non-traditional technique and share their methods in these pages. In short, using nothing more than the shop staple yellow glue and an iron, the major mysteries of veneering are solved. Of course, there's much more to veneering than the glue; the order of application, making tight seams, and trimming techniques are also covered.

For the more adventurous, Frank Pollaro shows how to manipulate matching sheets of veneer to create fantastic patterns, such as diamonds, reverse diamonds, and sunbursts. These aren't techniques for the faint-hearted, but by no means are they out of reach of most woodworkers.

As with all techniques, complex and simple, getting advice and instruction from woodworkers who really know their stuff is the best first step. From there, informed practice will help you internalize those lessons and turn what you know into what you can do. Knowing how to veneer opens huge new vistas in woodworking, giving you far greater choice in using sheet goods and cheaper substrates in construction and the potential for some really stunning visual effects.

VENEERING A TABLETOP

by Michael Burton

Sitting in a dimly lit room, the old pool table looked more or less sound. Some of the veneer had started to peel, and the owner was anxious to know whether the table could be repaired. "Of course it can," I told him.

Later, when I took the table and my bravado into the shop, it was a different story. Lots of veneer had to be replaced. I started to worry about the hot hide glue I'd always used for veneering. The glue holds down veneer just fine, but wood that isn't veneered on both sides can warp. I didn't see a way to get the table apart to get at both sides of all the pieces, at least not easily. I was stuck.

Before long, I was experimenting with aliphatic resin glue. I learned that once dried, this glue can be reactivated with a household iron to form a very good bond. Best of all, veneer applied this way to only one side of the workpiece doesn't cause any distortion. The pool table was salvaged. Ever

since, I've been using this iron-on technique on everything from repairs to new tabletops as large as 7 ft. dia.

The technique is simple. Glue is applied to both the veneer and the ground (the material the veneer is glued to). After the glue has dried, the two materials are ironed together. The heat from the iron melts the glue and bonds the two surfaces.

You don't need any special or expensive equipment like bulky veneer presses or vacuum bags (mine is now gathering dust in a corner of the shop). Nor is it necessary to join several pieces of veneer together with veneer tape before covering a large surface; the seams are made as the sheets are applied. This technique works with wrinkled veneers, even burls and crotches, and it may save you the trouble of flattening such rare and beautiful woods before application.

Like any other technique, though, ironing down veneer has its quirks. If you've tried this approach, you know that heat produced by an iron can shrink the veneer, opening up seams and causing some checking if you're not careful. When used with a little forethought, however, these problems are minimal at worst. The keys to success are preshrinking the veneer before ironing it down, applying the glue in several thinned coats and cutting the seams as you go. This is the same approach I used to veneer a small game table that my shop was recently commissioned to make (see the photo on the facing page). The iron-on method worked perfectly, and I'll show you how I did it.

Test veneer for shrinkage, and repair any holes

Before thinking about glue, the veneer should be checked for heat tolerance. Some species can shrink dramatically under the heat that will be required to bond them with dry glue. To check, measure a piece of veneer across the grain, and then heat the wood with your iron at the three-quarter setting (see the photo at left on p. 142). After the veneer has cooled for a few minutes, measure again. If the shrinkage is significant, it's a good idea to pre-shrink all of the veneer you plan to use by thoroughly heating it with the iron. Even though the glue will swell the veneer when it's applied, pre-shrinking the material now reduces the chance of checks and open seams later.

If there are any defects in the veneer, such as holes or checks, now's the time to tape them on the face side. A number of woodworking suppliers sell veneer tape. It's just a strip of paper with adhesive on one side that you wet and stick down. When you're all done, you can scrape the tape off. It's not a good idea to use masking tape; heat from the iron will turn it into a gummy mess, and masking tape stretches.

The veneer tape will hold the veneer together and prevent the glue from reaching the face. If you're working with paper-backed veneer, which has a layer of paper bonded to the back side of the veneer, scuff the paper with 80-grit sandpaper before applying the glue. If you don't do this, the glaze on the paper can cause problems in getting an even glue coat.

Because I cut the seams as I go along, there's no need to fit the veneer precisely to the ground at this point. I lay out where the

Two coats of glue on both surfaces. The author uses a brush to spread thinned glue on the top of this game table.

seams will be on the ground with a sharp pencil and make sure that the pieces of veneer will cover the area with a little bit to spare. With these steps out of the way, I can apply glue to both the veneer and the ground.

Spread the glue in several coats

Glue thinned about 10% with water spreads easier and covers better than one coat straight from the bottle. I use either Titebond or Elmer's yellow glue, thinning it until it's the consistency of heavy cream. Complete coverage is important, and a brush works much better than a roller (see the photo at right below). A roller can leave air bubbles and an undesirable texture and is totally ineffective on wrinkled veneer.

Spreading glue on the ground is very straightforward—just brush on a good, even coat (see the bottom photo on p. 141). Before spreading glue on the veneer, it's a good idea to mist some water from a spray bottle on the face side. This will help eliminate curling caused by the moisture of the glue on the back. After the glue has been spread on the back side of the veneer, place the veneer on sticks so that air circulates around both sides.

If possible, stay with the veneer as the glue dries. If puddles form, spread them out with a putty knife or a scrap of plastic laminate. Make sure that edges that will be part of a seam are well-covered with glue. After the first coat of glue has dried (dry means that all of the creamy white color has been

Getting the shrink out. Because some veneers shrink dramatically during the bonding process, the author starts by pre-shrinking all the veneer with the iron at a three-quarter setting.

Thin the glue, and paint it on. Aliphatic resin glue thinned about 10% with water spreads easily with a brush, eliminating the bubbles that can occur with a roller.

Bond first, trim later. With layout lines drawn on the tabletop, the author bonds the first piece of padauk veneer in the pattern. He keeps the iron away from edges that need trimming.

A sharp linoleum knife works best. With a straight-edge and a linoleum knife, the author trims the edge of the first piece of veneer. Knife marks are extended beyond the edge as a reference for trimming the next piece of veneer accurately.

replaced with a transparent light yellow), feel the surface. If it has become rough, sand lightly with 80-grit paper. Then put a second coat of glue on both the veneer and the ground.

Some species of veneer and some ground materials, such as the raw edge of medium-density fiberboard (MDF), may require a third or even a fourth coat. The object is to have a smooth, glossy, transparent film of glue that looks a little like a thick coat of varnish. Veneer will have a leather-like feel when it's properly coated with glue.

Once you have enough glue on both surfaces and it has dried, pass a sanding block

with 80-grit paper lightly over the ground and, if possible, the veneer. This will knock the top off any dust, coagulated glue or whatever may have settled on the glue as it was drying. Anything that the sandpaper won't smooth out should be cut off with a sharp knife or a chisel.

It's just like ironing your shirt

Now it's time to iron down the first piece of veneer. Position a rough-cut piece of veneer so that it overlaps any seams by $1/4$ in. or so (how much overlap you can afford will depend on the veneer and your pattern, but don't leave any less than $1/8$ in.). Heat, resid-

For wrinkled veneer, cut the seam in place. Heat can distort the edges of some veneers, so the author may choose to cut a clean edge once the second piece of veneer is mostly bonded.

ual moisture and wrinkles can often distort the veneer as it's bonded. This is the reason I prefer trimming after the bonding process. With the iron turned up about halfway, use the tip to tack the veneer in place. Then with slow, circular motions, proceed to bond this first piece of veneer, staying $1/4$ in. or so away from areas that will be trimmed later (see the left photo on p. 143).

How hard do you press the iron? Don't break the handle! But remember that the heated glue is plastic, not fluid, so the more pressure the better. There is no law against using two hands. You will often hear clicking sounds as you iron. These are small spots pulling loose. You should iron until the clicking stops. Keep the iron moving—don't linger in any spot. Overheating the glue will destroy its bonding characteristics.

Should you encounter a real stubborn wrinkle, moisten the area with a damp cloth, and iron it immediately. Don't give the area a chance to swell. The added moisture and heat will cause the area to com-

press, and the steam will penetrate the veneer to aid the glue bond. I've heard the suggestion that a steam iron be used for bonding. This works for single pieces and large sections of paper-backed veneer, but in a design with a lot of seams, the added moisture often can cause dimensional changes in the veneer that are completely intolerable. Keep your work as dry as possible.

Trim the first seam, then test the bond

With the first piece bonded, I trim the seams with a sharp linoleum knife, my tool of choice. I just think of it as a veneer saw with one tooth. And like a saw, it works best when you make the cut in a number of passes.

When cutting the seam, I let the knife overcut the veneer into the border areas (see the right photo on. p. 143). These marks will be used for lining up the straightedge for trimming the next piece. Should you encounter areas of waste that have been accidentally bonded, cut them loose with a sharp chisel (a dogleg is excellent for the job). If the glue has been removed from the ground, re-spread those spots.

After trimming, you may wish to check the bond. I always do. With your fingernail or a stiff brush, go over the surface and listen for a hollow sound indicating that the veneer isn't bonded. Then I moisten the veneer with a damp cloth. Loose spots will manifest themselves as bubbles. If you are working in a quiet area, the veneer often will talk to you. A clicking sound will be heard as the bubbles pull themselves loose. If any loose spots are detected, use the tip of the iron and a little extra pressure to bond them, and then pass the iron over the entire piece to dry it.

Cutting and fitting the next piece

That first piece is now well-bonded. In fact, if you tried to pry it up, the veneer would take chunks of the MDF with it. The next step is to rough-cut the second piece and position it for bonding. If you are working with flat veneer that doesn't seem to wrinkle much under heat, you may wish to precut the second piece and shoot the edge with a sanding block. If this is the case, let the piece overlap the first by about 0.01 in. (about the thickness of a matchbook cover). Then bond the second piece of veneer, staying about 1½ in. back from the seam.

The secret to a tight seam is that little extra you've allowed. Take that 0.01 in. of overlap, and buckle the veneer slightly so that the seam edges are butted together. A piece of $^3/_{16}$-in. steel or brass rod pushed beneath the second piece of veneer near the edge is a great help (see the photo at right). If the trimmed seam is a little ragged, carefully pass a sandpaper block over it. And if you are the type who wears a belt and suspenders simultaneously, you also may wish to brush a light coat of fresh glue on the edge of the veneer. I have often done this where I feared the veneer shrinking and the seam opening up.

After the pieces are butted together, withdraw the rod, and iron down the buckled seam (see the photo at right). Position the iron so it spans the whole seam. The veneer often splits when the tip of the iron rides the center of the buckled area, so make sure the entire area is covered with the sole of the iron. A joint made in this manner places a great amount of pressure at the seam and is highly unlikely to open up.

If your veneer is wrinkled, the procedure is slightly different but gets you the same result. Let the second piece overlap the first by at least ¼ in.; then iron it down except for the 1½ in. next to the seam. After the veneer is down, trim the edge to be seamed with the first piece.

Make the cut so the second piece overlaps the first by about 0.01 in. (see the photo on the facing page). Cut through the top piece only. I use a scrap of plastic laminate to protect the bottom piece of veneer. This is not a double-cut. Do I have to tell you to work carefully? You have only one chance.

Test the surface with a damp cloth

I use this one-piece-at-a-time approach until I've covered the top with veneer. I make sure the veneer is well-bonded by

Secret for a tight seam. For a seam that won't pull open from the heat of the iron, the author cuts the second piece of veneer 0.010 in. wide. Then he buckles it over a piece of $^3/_{16}$-in. rod so that the edges meet.

Iron down the hump. Working from one end and withdrawing the rod as he goes, the author presses down the seam. It will stay tight.

dampening the surface with water and looking for bubbles. Bubbles detected now are easy to fix with an iron. If you find one later, don't panic. A product called Brasive (Mohawk Finishing Products Co., 4715 State Highway 30, Amsterdam, NY 12010-7417; 518-843-1380) introduced through a pin hole in the bubble will reactivate the glue and bond the veneer without reheating.

EASY VENEERING WITH A HOUSEHOLD IRON

by Mario Rodriguez

Ironing on veneer is simple and quick even on curves like this apron. First apply yellow glue to both the substrate and the veneer; let them dry. Then place the two together, and reactivate the glue with an ordinary iron.

Being able to veneer can dramatically extend the scope of projects available to a woodworker. You can take veneer, a beautiful but unstable material, and apply it to a solid, flat substrate. You can also repeat or book-match patterns for a spectacular effect. But what's the best way to glue down the veneer and keep it down?

Mentioning traditional techniques of hot hide glue and a veneer hammer produces accelerated pulses and sweaty palms for most woodworkers. In my veneering workshops when students get over their initial fear of gluing veneer, they are okay.

But when I visited former apprentice Ken Vigiletti, he turned me on to another way of applying veneer using waterproof yellow glue and a household electric iron (see the photo on the facing page). At first, I was skeptical. But after seeing a demonstration, I was anxious to get back to my shop to give the technique a try. And the project I had in mind—a small half-round hall table that I wanted to cover with sycamore veneer—was perfect because veneer would enhance the table's form (see the photo at right).

Vigiletti's demonstration was not the first time I'd seen veneer adhered with an iron. The technique also appeared in *Fine Woodworking*. But in that article, the author applied white glue to the substrate, and then he immediately ironed on the veneer. With that method, the veneer can slide on the wet glue, causing misalignment and gaps at the seams. By contrast, when you heat the dry glue through the veneer, it adheres in place right away. And water is less likely to evaporate out of the glue and through the veneer, causing bubbles.

About the adhesive

The main appeal of veneering with yellow glue is that many of us use it daily. With yellow glue, you don't have to worry about water-to-glue ratios, soaking time, temperature, hammering pressure or the mess associated with hide glue. And by using an ordinary iron, there's no need for a vacuum bag, an expensive press or any complicated clamping cauls. But because I wasn't keen about the idea of having to redo the veneer if the bond failed, I was still hesitant about heating waterproof glue with an

Veneer can emphasize a table's form. To bring out this table's traditional shapes, like tapered Federal-style legs, the author veneered it with sycamore. The table is suitable for an entrance hall or this formal dining room at the historic Peach Grove Inn in Warwick, N.Y.

iron. So I asked one of *Fine Woodworking's* regular contributors, Chris Minick, about the process. Minick, a research chemist, heartily endorsed the technique (see the box on p. 149).

Even before talking to Minick, I was attracted to the prospect of ironing veneer over waterproof glue for a couple of reasons. In situations where the wood will be exposed to moisture, such as in a sink cabinet or in a vanity for a bathroom, the veneer isn't likely to come loose. Also, once this type of glue is cured, it isn't sensitive to common finishing solvents, so finishing shouldn't affect the veneer bond.

Another advantage of this method is that you can glue down burl or crotch veneer without getting glue stains, which can cause finish delamination and uneven staining. When you glue down these veneers using a press, the glue bleeds through. This is

Stabilizing and gluing veneer—With a scrapwood backup, Rodriguez rolls glue onto the back of the veneer. By spraying water on the face of the veneer, he keeps the piece from curling. He has already smoothed the front of the apron and coated its surface with glue.

Scraping the veneer leaves a clean, smooth surface. Once the glue is cured and the veneer is set, the author uses a scraper to remove skid and scorch marks left by the iron. He keeps the scraper even and the strokes light to prevent the burr from digging into the surface.

because of the capillary action caused by the high percentage of end grain. Unless you use hide glue, the glue stains are nearly impossible to remove. However, by allowing the yellow glue to set up beforehand, you create a barrier near the surface that minimizes the bleed-through.

While I was talking to Minick, I learned of another technique that prevents the glue from bleeding through onto the face of the veneer. First seal the back side with shellac (use a 3-lb. cut). Once the shellac is dry, apply the glue and wait for it to dry. Then you can iron the veneer. Minick, who used the method on some quilted mahogany veneer, said that the shellac undercoat works well because shellac is thermoplastic, just like the glue and just like the burn-in repair sticks that furniture repairers and restorers use. And, if you get a dab of shellac on the veneer face, no big deal. Shellac is a great sealer; it's compatible with virtually any finish.

Cutting and taping the veneer

On the table project, I started by veneering the tapered legs (the legs made good practice before I did the top) and ended with the more difficult curved apron. I cut veneer for the legs using a sharp chip-carving knife. When veneering the top, I used narrow strips of veneer tape along the seam, and I reinforced the joint with shorter straps of tape running perpendicularly. Before gluing, I also taped all the cracks, which is especially important if you're using curly veneer. To see if there are any splits, hold the veneer up to a light. If there are any cracks of light, even slightly suspect areas, tape them.

Some veneers, like burls and crotches, require a substrate veneer laid 90° under the face veneer. This underlayment absorbs the movement of the face veneer and prevents tiny surface checks. Because of the relatively straight grain and the $1/28$ in. thickness of the sycamore veneer (most veneer is $1/64$ in. thick), I omitted this step on my table.

Applying the glue

To apply the Titebond II glue, I used a small paint roller with a short nap. I heavily coated both the substrate and the back of the veneer. Before setting the veneer to dry, I sprayed the face side with a little water to minimize any curl (see the top photo on the facing page). One thing to remember when you're working with veneer: What you do to one side, do to the other. In this case, the water mimics the glue.

Ironing the veneer

After setting down the veneer to dry for about 30 minutes, I placed the veneer with some overhang all around. Then, using a steam iron on the cotton setting, I pressed the veneer firmly and worked from the center out. I kept the pressure steady and the iron moving slowly. Looking for any gaps or open seams, I went over the veneer several times, allowing the iron to linger over any trouble spots. If you leave too much overhang on the veneer, the edges could curl away from the substrate, preventing a clean, tight job. To remedy this, limit overhang to $\frac{1}{8}$ in., and apply steam from the iron. The steam causes the veneer to expand on the face side, which allows it to lie flat again.

The iron left some light skid and scorch marks, but these were easily scraped off later after the glue cured (see the bottom photo

on the facing page). On larger areas, I work from the center out toward the edges to avoid creating bubbles or creases. But I've learned that every veneer behaves differently—even within the same species. So on certain jobs, you may want to iron the edges first. Experiment on scrap to see.

The heat from the iron should drive out excess moisture from the glue, which might otherwise bubble up under the veneer. Steam also works to temporarily release the veneer when you want to reposition it or when you need to iron out blisters and bubbles.

On my table project, the veneer was large enough to cover the apron in one piece, but often I have to join narrow pieces to span a larger surface. You can shoot and tape the seams prior to gluing, and then treat the assembly as one piece. Or you can lay the veneer one piece at a time, and cut your seams in place. You do this by overlapping the second piece onto the first and cutting through both of them. After passing your saw or knife over the seam several times, lift the top waste piece away from the seam.

Trimming veneer

Saw off the veneer leaving a little overhang to protect the edges. The author drags his veneer saw along the tabletop, leaving about 1/32 in. excess.

File and then scrape the surface flush, so the corner will be tight. After Rodriguez files the veneer edges level with the leg, he scrapes them smooth.

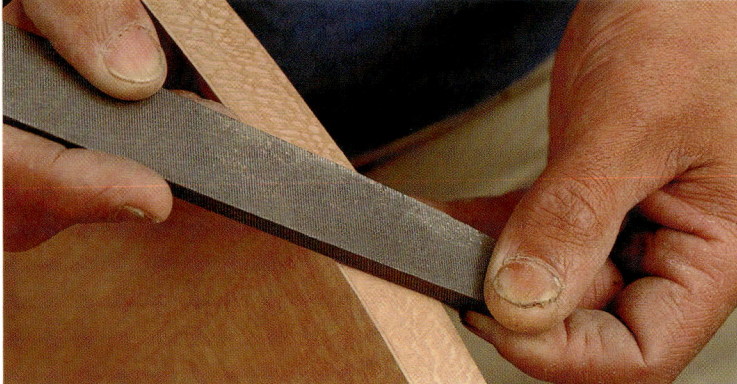

Chamfer adds a finishing touch—Using a smooth file, the author bevels the veneer edges, which eases and protects the table's corners and helps to disguise the seams.

Then gently lift the edge of the top sheet, and remove the waste strip from the bottom piece of veneer. If you can't lift the veneer, use a bit of steam from the iron to loosen up things. When both waste strips are removed, press the seam firmly. After ironing, apply veneer tape lengthwise down the seam, and place tape straps across the seam (which prevents the seam from creeping open). Leave the tape in place for 24 to 48 hours.

Trimming the veneer

To trim the veneer for the hall table, I used a sequence of hand tools. First I cut the veneer with a veneer saw, as shown in the top photo at left. I prefer a French veneer saw (which is available from the Garrett Wade Co. Inc., 161 Avenue of the Americas, New York, N.Y. 10013-1299; 800-221-2942) because its teeth point toward the center of the blade arc from both ends, which lets me score the veneer before beginning the cut. And because the handle is directly alongside the blade, a French veneer saw gives me better control than the more common offset-handle veneer saws.

Next, paying close attention to the direction of the veneer's grain, I use a block plane to trim the veneer almost flush with the adjacent surface. For this job, I use a Lie Nielsen block plane. And rather than risk tearing the veneer or digging into the wood, I leave the veneer edge proud. After planing, I use a 10-in.-long second-cut file to level the veneer to the substrate. I work from the edge into the veneer so that I don't chip it, and I lift the file on each return stroke.

Then I use a Sandvik scraper to smooth out the file marks, as shown in the center photo at left, while again noting the direction of the grain. The scraper leaves a clean surface that will ensure tight, almost invisible, seams. By keeping about three-fourths of the scraper on the work, I prevent the scraper's burr from rolling over the edge.

After gluing veneer to the adjoining surface and allowing it to dry, I repeat the above steps to trim the veneer where it meets at the corner. Finally, I slightly bevel the edge of the veneer at the joint using a smooth file (see the bottom photo at left).

VENEER MATCHING: FROM SMALL SHEETS, GREAT PATTERNS

by Frank Pollaro

There was a time when I couldn't imagine using veneer for anything more than covering the raw edges on plywood. Then a special table came along. I thought it might be nice to do something besides my usual solid-wood glue-up with an occasional inlay.

I had a local veneer supplier make an ebony sunburst for the tabletop. When the top arrived, I felt such admiration for the craftsman who had so perfectly arranged those 20 pieces of ebony veneer into a brilliant star. But besides admiration, I was determined to do the veneer work myself next time.

After ordering some veneer and reading up on veneering, I began cutting, arranging and pressing some basic veneer matches. Two years and several hundred square feet of veneer later, I cut my first 16-piece sunburst match for a tabletop. It turned out beautifully, but it did take some time.

Since then, I've worked increasingly with veneers and done many sunburst matches as well as plenty of simpler matches. I've learned a few things in the course of this work that make veneer matching easier and the results more consistently successful. You

BOOK-MATCH

FOUR-PIECE MATCH

DIAMOND MATCH

REVERSE-DIAMOND MATCH

Four simple matches make the most of smaller leaves of veneer. A book-match works best with veneers that have asymmetrical grain or figure patterns because the match creates symmetry. For the same reason, a four-piece match is best-suited for burls and other similarly wild-figured veneers. Diamond and reverse-diamond matches are most impressive with straight-grained veneers.

Practice pays off. The author so admired a sunburst veneer match he ordered from a local supplier that he taught himself how to make his own. It took some practice, but now he can make patterns like this tabletop in crotch mahogany.

don't have to tackle anything complicated to enjoy veneering. The figure, color and diversity of the veneers that are now available is breathtaking. Here are some techniques that have helped me.

The basic principle

The eye doesn't notice the precise width of a sheet, or leaf, of veneer, but the eye will notice sloppy asymmetry or poorly matched grain lines. That's why it's more important to make sure the grain lines in a pattern meet cleanly or are aligned in an attractive manner than it is to have all of the pieces of a pattern exactly the same size. This is the secret to a successful veneer match.

I usually pick an obvious mark, like a swirl, pin knot or area of particularly remarkable grain, and keep this mark the same distance from the edge of each leaf of veneer. That way, a pattern looks balanced or symmetrical throughout a match, regardless of whether it's a simple book-match or the most complex sunburst.

Book-matches and four-piece matches

A book-match is when two leaves of veneer are opened from a common edge, as you would open a book (see the top left photo on p. 151). Book-matching is best done with veneers that are obviously asymmetrical: Two veneer leaves opened so they look like mirror images of each other form a symmetrical, balanced whole.

When four leaves of veneer are book-matched and then book-matched again, perpendicular to the first seam, the result is a four-piece match (see the top right photo on p. 151). Burls and odd patterns commonly are used for a book- or four-piece match.

Diamond and reverse-diamond matches

The most sophisticated matches commonly used for square shapes are the diamond and reverse diamond. These are best-suited for straight-grained or striped woods. For a diamond match, the grain is positioned parallel to the four outside edges of the square (see the bottom left photo on p. 151). For a reverse diamond, the grain is perpendicular to the outside edges (see the bottom right photo on p. 151).

Creating a diamond or reverse diamond match is not an obvious process like a book- or four-piece match. For either the diamond or reverse diamond, I begin by cutting the four component pieces, each slightly longer than a finished side of the match and slightly wider than half of the match. I cut angles at 45° to the grain on two of the four pieces from the center of a long side to an opposite corner (see step 1 in the drawing on p. 154). Then I place one of the cut quarters over another uncut piece of veneer (this will be the quarter adjacent to it), carefully aligning the two pieces to get a 90° corner (step 2 in the drawing). I mark the second piece with a sharp pencil, cut it using a veneer saw and a good straightedge and then tape the two pieces together with veneer tape. I repeat the process with the other two pieces.

What I have now are two L-shaped pieces. I draw a line diagonally across the corners and then cut along that line, leaving a right triangle that is half of the match (step 3 in the drawing). This half is then laid over the other, grain lines are aligned and the bottom piece is marked and cut to form the second half of the square. Finally, the two halves are taped together to complete the match (step 4 in the drawing).

The sunburst match

By far, the most beautiful of all matches is the sunburst (see the photo on the facing page). It is most often used for round tables. But it also works well for squares, ovals, quarter- and half-rounds and arcs, which make beautiful headboards for beds.

Laying out, cutting and arranging the wedges

To make a sunburst match, I determine how many leaves of veneer I need. For the best results, they must be sequential leaves. That is, the leaves must be in the same order as they were sliced off the log, so grain variations are subtle and occur only gradually with each successive leaf in a stack, or book, as it's called. I usually make sunbursts using eight, 10, 16, 20 or 32 leaves (see the drawing on p. 155).

I decide how many leaves I need by multiplying the diameter of the desired circle by pi (3.14 is close enough) and then dividing this number by the width of my veneers. For example, for a round table, 30 in. dia., I'd multiply 30 in. by 3.14 and divide that number by the width of my veneers (say, 7 in.). In this case, the number of leaves I'd need to complete the circle is about 13½. I can't round the number down; therefore, I aim for 16 leaves because I have made 16-piece matches before, so I have a template to speed layout.

The templates are simple to make: For eight-, 16- and 32-piece matches, I halve a circle, halve the half and so on. I make the template just slightly wider (¹⁄₁₆ in. is about right) than the exact angle of each piece so that when half of the circle is assembled, I'll have slightly more than half of a sunburst. That way, I can tape up the two halves separately, and then trim each half with a straightedge. The two halves can be joined to form a complete circle. But I'm getting ahead of myself.

After I've established the number of leaves in my sunburst and made a template, I number each leaf in sequence. I preview what the finished sunburst will look like when it's assembled, so I know where to cut the individual sheets of veneer. I do this by taping two pieces of mirror together to create an adjustable angle, which I set on edge on one leaf in the match. By adjusting the angle to match the template and then moving the mirrors around, I can see the whole match before I make the first cut (see the

Creating a diamond or reverse-diamond match _____

The cutting and taping sequence is the same for diamond and reverse-diamond matches. The only difference is that the grain is oriented perpendicularly to the outside edges for a reverse diamond (below left) and parallel to the outside edges for a diamond (below right). Mark individual leaves as shown.

Reverse-diamond match

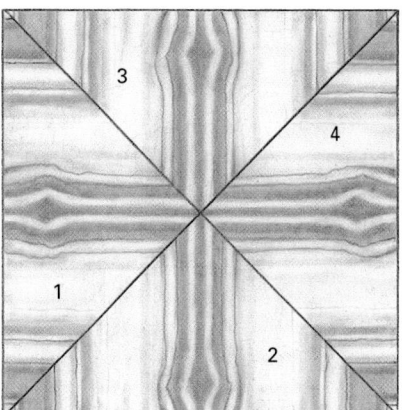

Diamond match

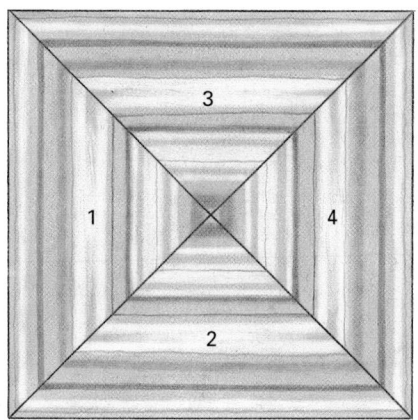

Step 1
First cut opposing leaves from their midpoints to the opposite corners.

Step 2
Now lay the cut half of #1 over #2. Align grain as well as you can, and then mark and cut #2. Tape these two pieces together. Repeat steps 1 and 2 with pieces #3 and #4.

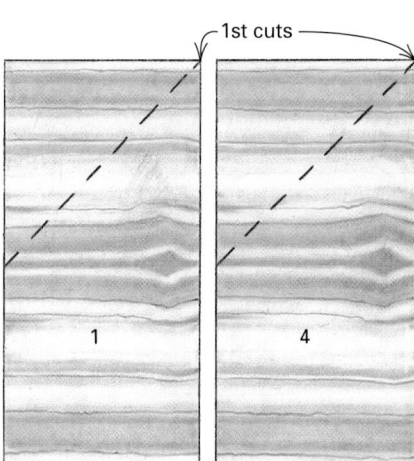

— 1st cuts —

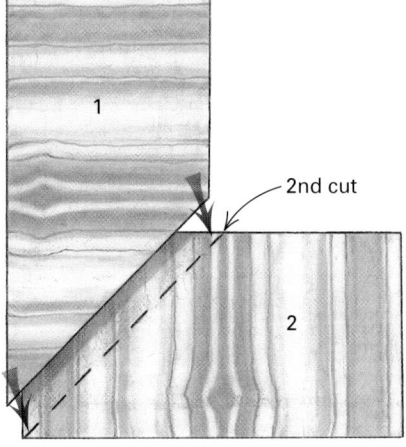

2nd cut

Step 3
Cut diagonally across L-shaped piece to create a right triangle. This is one-half of the match.

Step 4
Lay section #1-2 over section #3-4. Mark and cut as in step 3. Tape the two halves together, and you're done.

3rd cut

Waste

4th cut

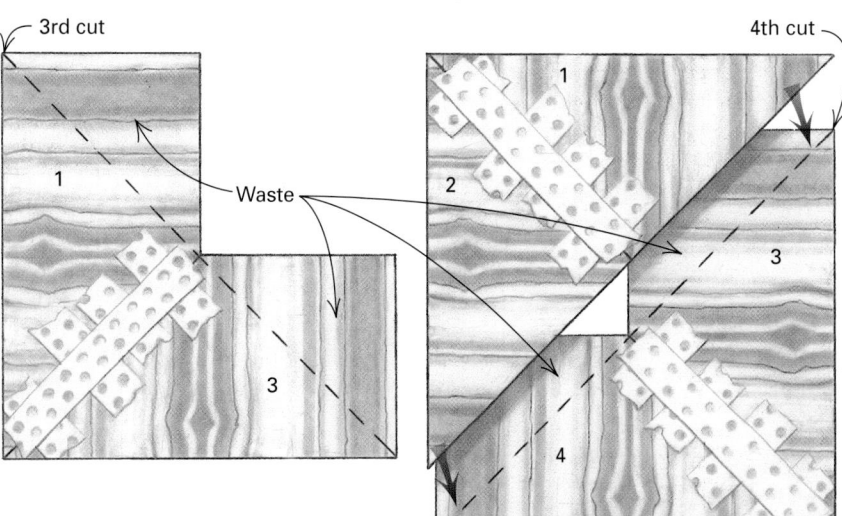

top photo on p. 156). I can be sure to get exactly the effect I'm looking for.

When I like what I see, I double-check that the space between the mirrors corresponds to the template, and then I trace along the inside edges of both mirrors. The next step is to cut one edge of this piece, using a reliable straightedge and a freshly sharpened veneer saw (see the center photo on p. 156). I now have a leaf of veneer with only one side of the wedge-shaped section cut. I lay this leaf on each of the remaining leaves and mark along the cut edge. This ensures that each section will be taken from the same place in each leaf, so I get the same effect I saw in the mirror. When all the leaves are marked, I cut along the marked lines. Now I take the template, mark the second side of the angle onto each of the pieces and cut them.

The next step is crucial, but not at all intuitive. If the leaves are laid out in sequence (one to 16, for example), then number one would be right next to number 16. With that layout, changes in the figure from leaf one to leaf 16 could be subtle or glaringly obvious. A knot might pierce a stack of veneer leaves at an angle, and the resulting sunburst would look as though it spiraled, an asymmetrical, not very pleasing effect.

To make the sunburst appear more balanced, I take the leaves out of chronological order and then assemble them in a sequence that eliminates any huge jump between leaves (see the drawing at right). The improvement may be subtle, but it's worth doing.

With the sequence established, the last decision I need to make is whether I want a pinwheel or a book-matched sunburst. In a pinwheel sunburst, the leaves are arranged with all the same faces up, and the resulting pattern looks like, well, a pinwheel. In a book-match sunburst, alternate leaves are flipped to create a running book-match. I lay out a sunburst both ways before I decide.

Taping and preparing the sunburst for the press

I tape the wedge-shaped sections across the seams every 5 to 6 in. and then over most of the length of the seam. To align

Laying out a sunburst _____

By positioning veneer leaves as shown, you can eliminate any abrupt changes in figure between leaves. This will keep the pattern looking more balanced throughout.

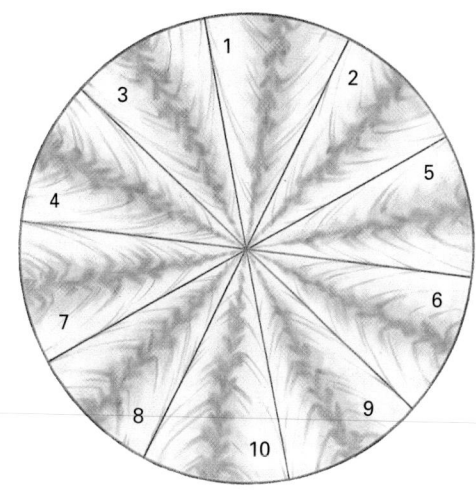

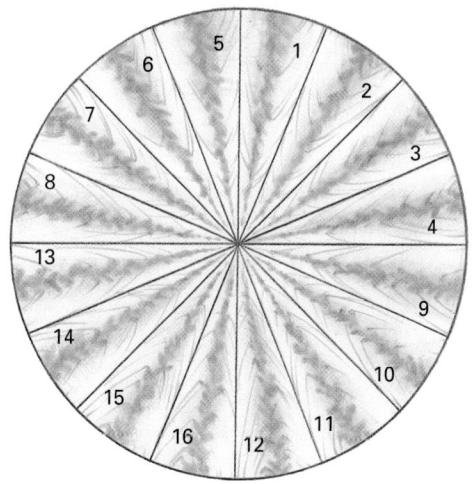

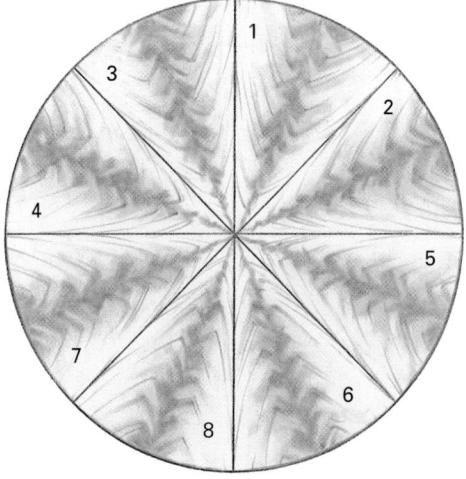

Laying out the top

Preview a whole sunburst on one leaf of veneer. By using a pair of hinged mirrors (duct tape will hold them together), the author can see how a sunburst will look before the first leaf has been cut.

A razor-sharp saw is essential for cutting heavily figured veneers like this crotch mahogany. A heavy straightedge with a fairly high side guides the saw and keeps it perpendicular to the veneer.

A template reduces layout time while improving accuracy. Even if you're only planning to do one sunburst, the time spent making a template will be well worth the effort.

the sections, I stop taping just shy of the center so that I can see where all the points come together (see the top two photos on p. 157).

I assemble the two halves of the match separately. Then I lay a straightedge across the edge of the first half so that the straightedge just touches where the points of veneer converge, and there's an even wedge of veneer to cut off to the left and right of center. There should be about $1/4$ in. on both sides at the perimeter of the half-circle. I trim carefully (see the second photo from the bottom on the facing page) because thin strips are prone to tearout. Then I repeat for the other half. I tape the two halves together, being particularly careful to line up the centers of the two halves. The match is complete (see the bottom photo on the facing page).

The sunburst should be pressed to the substrate as quickly as possible, particularly when using figured veneers such as crotch mahogany. These figured veneers tend to dry out unevenly, causing them to lift in places and making them difficult to press. If you can't get the match in the press the same day that you assemble it, make sure you cover the match with plastic (garbage bags work great for this), and weight it heavily.

If the sunburst is lifting off the table in the middle when it's uncovered, spray a light mist of water with a little glycerin (I dilute the glycerin 10 to one) near the outside edge. Allow the match to flatten for a few minutes before pressing. If the sunburst is lifting around the edges, spray the middle area, which will help prevent it from cracking once in the press. When I do press the sunburst, I make sure I also press a piece of backing veneer on the opposite side of the substrate. This equalizes the forces of wood movement and ensures the tabletop will stay flat. The backing veneer need not be the same highly figured wood.

Cutting and taping a sunburst match

Tape across the seams every 5 in. to 6 in. and then all the way along the seams. Stop just shy of the center, so you can see where all the points come together.

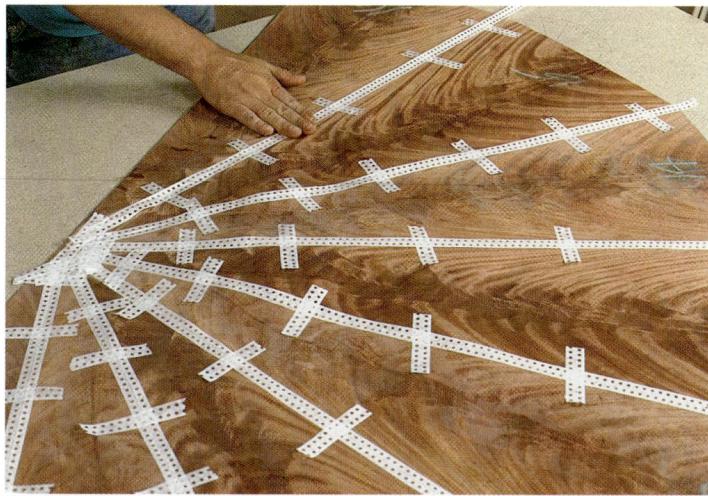

Paper veneer tape scrapes off easily after the veneer is bonded to the substrate. And it won't tear the veneer fibers like other kinds of tape.

Careful trimming with a veneer saw yields a perfect half-circle. The author sizes his templates, so half the match is slightly larger than a half-circle This allows him to trim thin wedges off each side and not have to worry about the two halves of the match falling short of making a full circle.

Rolling the tape with a veneer roller helps achieve a flat pressing. Make sure the edge of one leaf doesn't overlap an adjacent leaf. This prevents edges from breaking off in the press or a veneer leaf not adhering because it wasn't touching the substrate.

EIGHT

Inlay

Simple veneering, as complex and perhaps intimidating as it seems to a beginner, is only one member of a much larger family of techniques that use veneer. These include the many types of inlay and marquetry, where you can decorate flat surfaces of solid stock with anything from simple patterns to wildlife. These techniques aren't simple, but certainly not impossible, or really that difficult. All complex things can be broken down into several simple components. Herein lies the key to learning complex techniques: break them down. Chances are, you'll surprise yourself how much you already know.

String inlay is the art of pressing very thin pieces of veneer into grooves cut in solid wood. At a distance it looks like string has been delicately arranged on the piece, adding a quiet accent to simple designs. Garrett Hack demystifies the process, but reveals no sorcery in his toolbox except a jigged X-Acto knife. Two blades separated by a $1/16$-in. spacer cut perfect string inlay to any shape with templates.

The same lesson is evident in making geometric-design bandings. Each inch of banding might have 20 separate pieces. To put them together one by one would, of course, take an enormous amount of time and destroy eyesight. But Gary Straub breaks down the process into simple parts, showing how you never have to cut parts one by one.

Marquetry moves beyond a simple concatenation of basic woodworking jobs into the realm of artistic inspiration. Here your technique can be as good as anyone's, but it all depends on how you use it. The geometric patterns of most inlays require precision, along with some proportion, to look good. When making marquetry birds on the front of a dresser, however, a whole new set of expectations comes into play. No matter how precisely executed, the birds are only as lovely as their design. All woodworking partakes of the requirements of good design to some extent, but it is rarely as evident as in beautifully executed marquetry designs, for they require expression as much as top-notch technique.

STRING INLAY

by Garrett Hack

Early American furnituremakers used string inlay for much the same reason they used moldings—to outline and highlight parts of their furniture. In rooms where dim light was often the norm, the narrow bands of inlay emphasized the vertical lines of a table leg (see the photo on the facing page) or carried the eye around a curved apron. String inlay is most common on pieces from the Federal, or Hepplewhite, era (late 18th century through the first quarter of the 19th century). Designs from that period are among my favorites because the lines of the furniture are simple, yet the stringing adds high-style sophistication. That combination still works well today.

At one time, applying string inlay looked intimidating to me. Surprisingly, it's one of those techniques that looks more difficult than it really is. There are three main steps: cutting the groove, making the inlay and fitting the string to the groove.

Cutting the groove

I've always liked fine inlay, single-color strings no wider than $1/16$ in. and about $3/32$ in. deep. String this thin is very delicate in appearance and adds subtle detail, yet it's strong enough visually that it won't be missed. To inlay thin string, you must cut a very narrow groove in the workpiece. Most of the time, the best way to do this is with simple shop-made hand tools. I've come to distrust the power of a router, which can ruin work in an instant. Just the same, a template-guided router may be the best way of cutting grooves with complex curves. It's certainly the most efficient method, but you have to be prepared for the consequences of a momentary slip, because things happen quickly at 20,000 rpm. Each situation has its own best solution.

Cutting straight or gently curved grooves
Most grooves I cut can be made with a modified marking gauge. I removed the pin, used a bandsaw to cut a slot lengthwise on the beam of the marking gauge and inserted a cutter made from an old heavy-duty (about $1/16$ in. thick) hacksaw blade

(see the top photo on p. 162). The cutter, held in place with a pair of small nuts and bolts, is ground so that a tooth protrudes about $3/32$ in., with sides beveled at approximately 5° (see the top drawing on p. 162). The bevel helps the inlay go into the groove more easily. When grinding the tooth, I cool it often to avoid removing the temper, which would be easy with such a small profile. After grinding, I hone the four sides and bottom so that all of the edges are very sharp.

If you don't want to modify a marking gauge, you could pick up an old Stanley No. 66 beader or the reproduction of it now being made by Lie-Nielsen Toolworks (Route 1, Warren, Maine 04864; 800-327-2520). Either of these tools will hold a cut-

A look borrowed from an earlier era—Inlay only $1/16$ in. wide on the author's table is reminiscent of Federal pieces.

Tools for cutting straight grooves

Scratch tool cutter _____

Cutter is ground to a slight bevel (about 5° on each side) to make it easier to fit the inlay to the groove.

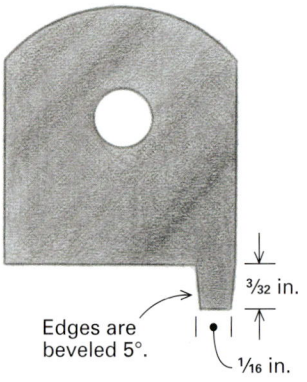

Edges are beveled 5°.

3/32 in.

1/16 in.

A scratch tool for cutting grooves parallel to an edge. The author made his from an old marking gauge and a piece of hacksaw blade.

Make grooves with light cuts. To use the tool, the author cants the tooth backward so that it scrapes lightly over the surface. With each pass, the tooth can be tilted more toward the perpendicular.

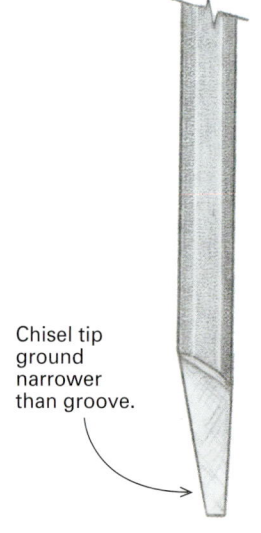

Custom chisel—Any good piece of tool steel can be made into a chisel for cleaning up the end of a groove.

Squaring up the ends of a groove ___

Chisel tip ground narrower than groove.

Square end of groove with the custom chisel. A marking knife and standard bench chisel are also used.

ter similar to the one I made, and Lie-Nielsen also sells cutter blanks.

It's easiest scraping with the grain, so I do these grooves first. I hold the fence of the tool tightly to the edge of the workpiece while rolling the tooth slightly back and scraping forward with smooth, light passes. The beauty of this scraping tool is that it cuts forward and backward. Once the groove is started, I deepen it, moving in both directions until the beam of the tool is rubbing against the work surface. The slight taper of the tooth helps keep the tool tracking down the groove. I keep the passes light, with the fence firmly pressed to the workpiece, and stop often to clear the tooth of accumulated scrapings. A light waxing of the fence and arm helps keep things running smoothly. It is not a rapid process, but part of what I enjoy most about woodworking is the quiet coordination of hand and eye.

My marking gauge also works well cross-grain as long as the tooth is sharp and the initial cuts are light with the tooth slanted well backward. Still, there is a tendency for the grain to rip a little in all but the hardest woods. It helps to use a sharp marking knife to score along the grain. I use a square or steel ruler as a guide and cut just inside of the lightly started groove. I repeat this when the groove is about half-cut. This decreases the resistance on the tooth, allowing it to cut more smoothly. The slight bevel of the tooth helps make the groove less fuzzy as it's deepened.

It's hard to scrape into the corners, so I use a sharp chisel, a marking knife and a second chisel I ground to fit easily within the groove (see the bottom photos and the drawing on the facing page). Working with these three tools, I can make sharp corners.

For gentle curves, I use the same modified marking gauge, as long as the fence has enough surface bearing on the workpiece to remain stable. Sometimes, I make bolder curves by attaching a specially curved fence to my marking gauge. Or sometimes, I mount the cutter from my marking gauge in a specially made scratch stock with a

Tools for cutting curved grooves

Cutting gentle curves

To cut an arc, use a set of dividers. File one tip of the dividers to a slightly beveled square profile, and then harden and hone it.

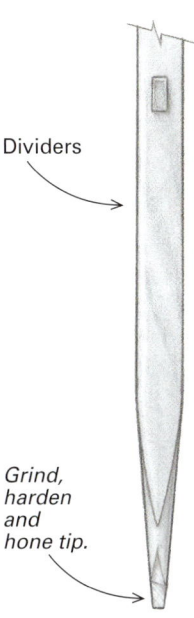

Dividers

Grind, harden and hone tip.

Cutting tight curves

Cutting a groove that doesn't follow an edge—An X-Acto hobby knife with two blades separated by a spacer outlines the groove around a plywood template. The author cleans out the waste with his custom chisel.

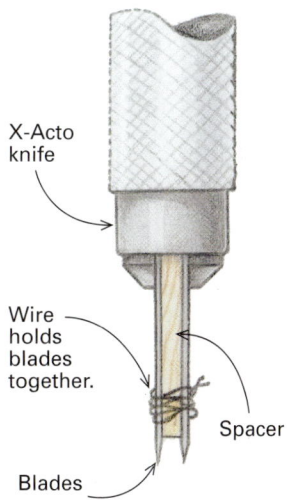

X-Acto knife

Wire holds blades together.

Spacer

Blades

Cutting and gluing in the string

Don't be fussy with the glue. Once the glue starts flowing, you have to move quickly because the moisture in the glue will swell the walls of the groove.

Rip strips of inlay on the tablesaw. Because the inlay stock is so thin, take it off on the waste side of the blade (above). Slice strips to ¼ in. or so with a knife and straight-edge. Plane to width with a block plane (below), beveling slightly to match the groove. Check the fit frequently.

A burnisher seats the strip of inlay securely. Tap the strip of inlay into the groove with a hammer and a block of wood. After removing most of the excess with a plane, make several passes with a burnisher. Apply more pressure with each pass until the inlay is seated.

fence whose curve matches the workpiece. With a curved fence, however, the tooth can't be tilted backward. This means that the tooth contacts the wood squarely, which calls for even lighter passes initially.

Cutting grooves for complex curves

There are situations where the curves are just too much for the modified marking gauge. To inlay a string line with complex curves, I generally resort to using a pattern and a specially made two-blade knife. This method also is useful anytime my design calls for a string line of some shape not parallel to an outside edge, such as outlining an oval reserve on a table apron (see the bottom photo and drawing on p. 163).

I make a pattern of thin hardwood or plywood to follow either the inside or outside edge of the intended string, whichever is easier. The knife is simply a pair of honed X-Acto blades, a thin spacer between them, mounted in a handle.

Lightly, at first, I score all around the pattern and then lift out the chips with my fine chisel. This process usually needs to be repeated a few times to get a sufficiently deep groove. For the final few passes, I hold the cutter from my marking gauge with my fingers and scrape carefully to get a groove of consistent depth and width.

Grooving with a router

Though I have done so a number of times, I don't like using a router to cut inlay grooves. Other woodworkers may not share my aversion. Outfitted with a template guide, the router's strength is its ability to follow a template of whatever shape. I've found it easier to follow an inside curve than an outside curve, so when I do use a router, I usually make a template with a cutout, remembering to account for the diameter of the template guide when sizing it. Router bits generally aren't available any smaller than $1/8$ in.

In these wider grooves, I usually inlay multicolored lines glued up from veneer. I have ground a high-speed-steel router bit down to a little less than $1/16$ in., for a single band of string. I rough out the groove with this bit and then clean it up with the cutter from my modified marking gauge.

Grooving an arc of a circle

To cut a groove that's an arc of a circle, I modified a pair of dividers, shaping the end of one leg to the same profile as the cutter from my modified marking gauge. The tooth scrapes a groove as the dividers are swung through an arc (see the top photo and drawing on p. 163).

Because the steel used for the dividers was soft, I hardened the tooth so it would stay sharp. I heated the tip to red hot with a propane torch and quenched it in water. I cleaned the tip with some fine sandpaper so the steel was shiny again; then I tempered the tip by reheating it until it was a light-straw yellow. I let it cool slowly and honed all edges of the tip.

I use the tool as I do the modified marking gauge, taking light passes at first to define the curve and reduce tearout in the cross-grain areas. Slanting the tooth back from the cut also helps, as does outlining the cut with a knife. The pivot point needs to be well-anchored. I sometimes can place the pointed leg in an area that will be inlaid later. If not, I glue down a small scrap of hardwood and chisel it off later or clamp a block to the piece I'm grooving.

Inlay materials

I use string inlay to outline or highlight, so I prefer to use a wood that contrasts with the primary wood. Black or white lines or some combination of the two work well because these colors hold better. Traditionally, holly has been used for white string because it stays the whitest and has almost no figure. I suspect white birch also has been used, but I prefer aspen, which stays nearly as white as holly and is so plentiful here in Vermont.

Ebony is another favorite of mine. I use it alone for black lines and in combination with aspen to make thicker stringing of alternating colors. Almost any wood that can be worked in thin dimensions can be inlaid, as can metals like brass and pewter.

When making string from solid stock, I rip it from a dressed board on the tablesaw to a dimension slightly wider than the groove it will fit. I find it safer and more accurate to pass the board against the fence, using the strips from the offcut side for the

String inlay deserves a good ending

A good way (and the traditional way) to terminate string inlay is to run it into a cuff inlay, which is a narrow band running around a leg just a few inches off the floor (see the photo below). A cuff inlay defines the transition point between the primary taper of a leg and a secondary taper for the foot.

Cuff inlay, which is a band encircling a leg near the floor, is the traditional termination for string inlay.

I vary the cuff's width, depending on the piece I'm making, but I always make the groove for it between 3/32 in. and 1/8 in. deep. This makes the cuff less vulnerable if it's kicked or bumped. I use a router and an adjustable fixture to create the groove (see the photo on the facing page).

The fixture compensates for taper

Because the leg is tapered, the trick in making the fixture is figuring out the angle that will create a continuous groove, with edges that line up perfectly all the way around. I do this by trial and error with a bevel gauge and pencil. Once I'm able to make a continuous pencil line around the leg, I use that bevel-gauge setting to position the front fence of the fixture and the plywood that will guide the router. I glue and tack these together.

After the glue has set up, I position the half-completed fixture so that the bottom edge of the plywood is properly situated to guide the router for the cuff groove (don't forget about the template guide). Then I clamp the fixture and another piece of scrap (the back fence) around the leg. I center a single screw through the plywood into the back fence and countersink the head. The fixture is ready to go.

Start the groove at the inside corner

I position the inside corner of the leg against the top edge of the front fence so that if the groove doesn't meet itself perfectly, the flaw will be less noticeable. Whenever possible, I use a template guide and bit that will cut the desired groove width in one pass. Occasionally, though, I have cut wider grooves in two passes by tacking a shim between the

inlay (see the top left photo on p. 164). This means the fence needs to be reset every pass. Rather than turning off the saw, waiting for the blade to coast to a stop and then measuring to get an offcut of precise thickness, I gauge it by eye. Small variations in thickness are unimportant because each piece is planed to fit its groove.

Fitting string to groove

I start with a piece of inlay that will protrude from the groove by as much as 1/8 in. A piece this wide is easier to hold while it's being planed to thickness and beveled. I mark one edge and designate it the top, so I can keep track as I'm planing and, later, when I'm gluing. The bevel, which should roughly match the groove, helps the inlay get started. And if I plane the inlay too thin, I can plane the bottom edge a bit so that the inlay will set deeper in the groove and snug up at the top. This is another good reason for leaving it wide when you start planing it.

Getting a good fit is simply a matter of trial and error. The inlay should fit snugly into the groove over its whole length. I miter the corners where inlays meet at an angle, using a chisel and splitting the angle by eye. When the strips have been beveled and planed to thickness, I rip them to about 3/16 in. with a knife and straightedge. That leaves no more than 3/32 in. of inlay above the surface of the workpiece. I also undercut edge of the plywood and the template bushing for the first pass. Then I remove the shim and make a second pass, with the template guide directly against the plywood.

I adjust the depth of cut in the front fence so the first complete pass is perfect. This groove helps me align the leg for subsequent passes. After each pass, I unclamp the leg and turn it toward me, lining up the routed groove in the leg with the one in the fixture. I'm careful to keep the orientation of the router the same on each pass, because router bases aren't always perfectly round.

Making, cutting and inlaying the cuff

I make my own inlay bands, laminating them from veneers or solid stock depending on the design. I start by gluing up a blank that will be ripped into strips of banding a little wider

A jig for cuff inlay—A scrap of plywood glued and nailed to a fence guides the router when cutting the wide groove for cuff inlay. Extra pieces on either side of the leg help locate the cuts and steady the router.

and thicker than the groove is wide and deep.

I cut the strips to length with a dovetail saw and miter them using a 45° shooting board and a wide chisel. Then I adjust the width of the banding with a block plane, creating a slight bevel on the edges. This helps when setting the banding into

the groove. I clamp each face, one at a time, using a small hardwood block as a caul. When the glue has set, I level all of the inlay with a sharp plane. If there's a secondary taper for the foot, I cut and plane it now.

the ends slightly and leave the inlay just a whisper long, so the ends will compress together when the inlay is tapped home.

As thin and flexible as inlay is, it sometimes won't make the bend when set into tightly radiused grooves without being soaked in water for a few minutes and bent around a form. I try to plan ahead when I have tight radii to inlay, so I can let the pieces dry overnight on the form before working with them.

Gluing in the string requires quick and careful work because the moisture in the glue swells the parts. I try to put a fine bead of glue in the groove using a whittled piece of scrap thinner than the groove (see the top

right photo on p. 164). It's not always a neat process, though. I quickly position the string and, working from one end to the other, lightly tap it in using a hammer and a block of scrap to protect the inlay strip.

With my block plane set for a moderate cut, I plane off most of the excess and then set the inlay with an oval burnisher (see the center right photo on p. 164). This snugs the inlay in place and works out any extra glue at the corners. When the glue has set, I level the whole surface with a sharp plane (see the bottom right photo on p. 164).

INLAY BANDINGS DRESS UP YOUR WORK

by Gary Straub

Inlay bandings are sliced from a board that has been made for that purpose. Cutting bandings on the bandsaw results in less waste than cutting them on the tablesaw. It's also much safer on the bandsaw because there's no danger of kickback or of the blade binding.

The simplest and most prevalent form of inlay is with strips of wood (bandings) as borders, but many woodworkers a shy way from using inlay bandings, thinking it too difficult a process. Though some bandings can be time-consuming and difficult to make, many are not. Inlay bandings range from simple string inlay (a thin strip of contrasting wood) to exceedingly complex creations with hundreds of pieces comprising a geometric design. I'll discuss the basics of making bandings and then the specifics of a few different types (see the top photo on the facing page).

To understand the process of making bandings, you need to see the banding three-dimensionally. Bandings are not made individually but rather as a board that will be sliced into many identical strips (see the photo below). The simplest of bandings, a solid strip of wood, is perhaps the easiest way of getting a feel for making banding. To make 10 bandings for a large tabletop, I wouldn't just randomly select 10 thin pieces of wood. Instead, I'd select a board I liked and cut 10 consecutive strips from it. This way, each of the 10 bandings is virtually identical, and the grain pattern—however

subtle—is repeated around the table. This technique is the same for any type of banding. For strips that consist of more than one piece of wood, though, you have to make a board, and to do that, you have to know how big to make it.

Sizing the banding

First decide how wide to make the face of the banding. Commercially available bandings come in a myriad of widths, from less than 1/16 in. to well over an inch. The right width of banding will depend on the style and scale of your project. I always try to match a banding width to one of my router bits, so I can easily use my plunge router to make an accurate groove for the inlay. If you need a banding that doesn't correspond to any available bits, two passes with a smaller bit will give you any width you like.

Commercial bandings are 36 in. long, but I make mine to fit the piece I'm inlaying. I usually make the board a little longer than the shortest measurement of the piece. For example, for a tabletop 40 in. by 80 in. with banding 1½ in. from the edges, I'd make the banding about 38 in. long (40 in. less 1½ in. at either end is 37 in.). On something small, though, like a box top, I sometimes make the banding as long as a side and an end combined. Of course, I often have to splice pieces together to get the length I need, but the idea is to create a length that neither falls just shy of a corner nor is so long that it's a pain to make.

The board's depth is determined by how many pieces you want to get out of it. Because I make only custom, one-of-a-kind furniture, I usually make the board just deep enough for the piece I am working on, plus a little extra in case of mistakes. To figure the depth, I add the thickness of the banding (I make mine 3/32 in. thick) and the width of my bandsaw's kerf (1/16 in. for the 3/8 in., 8 teeth-per-inch blade I use to resaw the bandings) and multiply that sum times the number of pieces I'll need, plus a couple of extras.

Designing and making banding

The next most simple type of banding after a plain strip of wood is a solid strip with a border of contrasting wood on each side (see samples 2 and 3 in the top photo). I resaw

An infinite variety of inlay bandings is possible. Your imagination is the only limit. As a rule, though, you should be sure borders of bandings consisting of a number of different woods contrast with the wood into which you're inlaying them. How these seven samples were each made is discussed in the text.

When gluing up straight from the saw, the author always uses the tablesaw outfitted with a good-quality finish blade.

the three pieces to approximate thickness and then run them through the planer to exact thickness—a ½-in. center with ⅛-in. borders in the case of the two bands pictured. My planer goes down to 3/32 in., so I don't need to rig up any special fixtures. Next I apply Titebond yellow glue and clamp the three pieces together with a thick board on each side to help distribute the clamping pressure. I use C-clamps set every 2 in.

A variation on this design, which looks more complicated than it is, is sample 5 in

Preparing, cutting and inlaying bandings

Inlaying bandings into a surface is only a matter of routing a groove the same width as the banding and gluing the banding in place. The tools needed are minimal, and the technique is basic.

The first thing I do is mark the corners where the outside edge of the bandings will go, so I'll know where to stop the router. The simplest way to do this is with a marking gauge. I use a gauge I've modified to accept an ordinary #2 pencil.

I chuck the correct router bit into my plunge router and set the depth of cut by using a drill bit ⅟₆₄ in. or ⅟₃₂ in. narrower than the thickness of the banding as a gauge. Setting the router on a flat surface, I lower the router bit until it just touches the surface. Then I put the drill bit between the depth-adjustment rod and the stop post. I lower the rod snugly against the drill bit and lock the rod in place. This method is accurate and leaves the banding just proud: It's easier to take off a little excess banding than it is to bring down the entire surface around the banding.

I put the edge guide on the router and set the distance using the marks that I penciled at each corner. Then I plug in the router and rout the groove all around, using my pencil marks as stop points.

If the banding goes in farther than my edge guide will allow, I use a Tru-Grip Clamp 'n' Tool guide (available in many woodworking catalogs) to guide my router. A straightedge and C-clamps also work. I determine where to place the guide by fastening it to a piece of scrapwood and routing a test groove. Then I measure from the edge of the groove to the guide to get my distance setting. Once I've routed the grooves, I square off the outside corners with a sharp chisel.

I start inlaying by cutting a miter on one piece (see the photo at left below) and fitting it into a groove with the mitered point touching the end of the groove. Next, if the piece extends past a corner at its other end, I mark where the next miter will be, indicate with a line the direction of the miter (so I don't cut it the wrong way) and I cut it. Then I put the mitered piece on top of the next piece to be cut, moving it around until I find a match. I mark it, cut it and continue to the next piece.

Where I need to splice pieces together for longer banding strips, I use either a butt joint or a miter, depending on the banding pattern. When inlaying bandings with geometric patterns, I sometimes reverse the pattern in the middle so that the corners will meet properly and be symmetrical.

If the banding is too tight for the groove, I just run it over a block plane mounted upside down in my vise (see the photo at right below). If I need to take more than one pass, I alternate edges to keep the banding symmetrical. If I cut a piece too long or if a miter is slightly off, I use a sharp chisel to pare off a sliver.

Once I've cut and fit all the pieces, I glue them in. I use Titebond, only putting glue down for one piece at a time and making sure there are no dry spots. I force the banding down with the side of a round mallet, squeezing out any excess glue, always working from the middle out and pressing hard. After the last piece is in, I roll it all again. If the fit is good, the bandings do not need any clamping. By tapping my fingernail on the banding all the way around, I can find any spots where the banding isn't all the way down. Once the glue is set, I scrape off the excess glue and handplane the bandings flush with the surface using a finely tuned plane with a very sharp blade. Now the piece is ready for final sanding.

A small miter box and a Japanese backsaw work well for cutting miters at corners and for splicing the banding. A Western-style backsaw also works just fine.

An inverted block plane with a very sharp blade is just the thing for shaving off tiny curls to get a piece of oversized banding to fit.

Cutting laminations at an angle and combining them imaginatively give you a whole other range of possibilities for bandings.

The author's wenge and mahogany shelving unit incorporates some of his own inlay banding, adding more visual interest.

the top photo on p. 169 and in the photo on p. 168. Instead of using one wide center strip, I resawed and planed two thinner strips of walnut and used a piece of dyed veneer (available from most veneer suppliers) in the center. Then I drilled centered holes on the drill press and took a dowel smaller than the diameter of the drilled holes to spread glue inside each hole, one at a time. Finally, I hammered home dowels I'd sized exactly by forcing them through a drill-bit gauge's $^{19}/_{64}$-in. hole.

The geometric patterns in samples 6 and 7 in the top photo on p. 169 are similarly easy to make. There's just one more step in the process, and a visualization leap you have to take. I started by laminating three pieces each of maple and walnut, $^{1}/_{2}$ in. by $^{3}/_{4}$ in. by 14 in. Then I jointed one side (of alternating maple and walnut) and planed the other to make them uniform after gluing. I cut the block into $^{1}/_{2}$-in. strips at 45° across the grain (see the bottom photo on p. 169) on the tablesaw. I always use a tablesaw outfitted with a finish blade to cut pieces that will be glued up without surfacing. I used the resulting blocks to make banding 7 in the top photo on p. 169.

There are a few tricks to working with diagonal pieces. To get length, you'll need to butt sections together. To do this, square up the end pieces, so you can more easily clamp the whole thing together lengthwise. Cut the two border pieces slightly shorter ($^{1}/_{8}$ in. or so) than the total length of the diagonal pieces. Apply yellow glue to the inside of both border pieces and to the juncture of every pair of diagonal strips. Clamp loosely across the width every few inches

with C-clamps, and squeeze the diagonal pieces together with a bar or pipe clamp. Now tighten the C-clamps.

Strip 7 in the top photo on p. 169 and the one I used in the shelving unit in the right photo above was made using this same technique, except I cut the diagonal strips at $^{1}/_{4}$ in. and reversed them on top of each other, making a four-piece lamination instead of three. I also used plastic-resin glue instead of Titebond because it takes more time to set, which is helpful when you're gluing several pieces at once. Many banding designs are possible with this method, using the same building blocks (see the left photo above). I made banding 4 in the top photo on p. 169 to create a similar look but without using a glued-up lamination. I used a piece of zebrawood that I cut on the diagonal, but this method will work with any wood that has prominent vertical stripes.

Sawing the bandings

Before cutting a board of banding into inlay strips, I first joint one edge, making sure it's square. Then I mark the top (perpendicular to the face) with a V to keep track of the order in which strips are cut. I cut the strips on my bandsaw (see the photo on p. 168). I prefer the bandsaw for cutting strips because there's less waste and because it's much safer than trying to cut the $^{3}/_{32}$-in. strips against the fence on a tablesaw—an operation you shouldn't consider. After I've cut a board into bandings, I put rubber bands around the pack to keep them from distorting until I'm ready to use them.

MARQUETRY STEP-BY-STEP

by Gregg Zall

At woodworking school, I was given the time and the confidence to stretch my cabinetmaking skills to the limit. I challenged myself to include graphic arts in my cabinets, which would combine my love of drawing and furnituremaking. Painting surfaces seemed a shame, though, because paint covers up the wood. Instead, I decided to use the natural colors of wood to create pictures with marquetry.

After a lot of trial, error and advice, I came across a method called double-bevel cutting, which gave me the small, accurate details that I wanted on my cabinets, like the birds across the drawer fronts in the cabinet shown below. There are no distracting gluelines in the finished piece.

How is it done? First tape two pieces of veneer together like a sandwich, and then cut out your design, as shown in the photo at left. The trick is that you cut the hole for the inlay and the inlay piece itself simultaneously, so any deviation in the cut is mirrored in both the inlay and the hole.

Because the cut is made at an angle, the inlay piece on the bottom of the sandwich comes out fractionally bigger, taking up the sawkerf and making a perfect fit when glued

Flawless marquetry may be easier than you think. The marquetry detailing across the drawers on the author's cabinet uses the natural colors of wood to paint a picture. The technique he uses ensures that pieces fit together correctly.

Tilt the table, not the saw. A plywood cutting table tilted at 8° creates the beveled edges of inlay and background pieces. The author moves a jeweler's saw straight up and down, not at an angle, and pulls the work into the saw to cut the patterns.

in, as shown in the drawing on p. 174. The bevel-edged inlay piece snugs down into the bevel-edged cutout just like the underside of a flat-head screw fits into a countersink. It's really not that hard to do. So if you're game, I'll walk you through it step by step.

Sawing your own veneer

I use my own hand-cut veneers for marquetry. One advantage is that I can pick the wood and figure. All the odd scraps of wood I couldn't bear to toss out are suddenly usable. I have my own favorites, which I've listed by color group in the chart above. Another advantage of cutting my own veneer is that the extra thickness makes the glue joints, and thus the work itself, stronger. I use a bandsaw equipped with a high fence to cut my veneers $\frac{1}{16}$ in. thick, as shown in the photo on p. 174.

I joint one face of the stock before sawing and then use the veneer just as it comes off the saw. The veneers need to be pretty consistent. Because every bandsaw blade cuts at a slightly different angle, it's essential to clamp a fence to the bandsaw table parallel to the natural drift of the blade.

Setting up a saw and angled table

If you want to try this marquetry technique and you don't have a scroll saw, try a jewel-er's saw with an 8-in.-deep throat (available from Frei and Borel, 126 2nd St., Oakland, Calif. 94607; 800-772-3456). A saw this size allows you to do a 6-in.-sq. design, and this saw is more than capable of producing beautiful work. I fitted mine with a longer handle, like the ones found on Japanese saws. And you'd better buy a few dozen blades because they break often.

There's a little trick to installing blades in a jeweler's saw. First insert one end of the blade in the collet by the handle. The teeth should point down toward the handle. Adjust the saw's frame length so that the top collet is $\frac{1}{8}$ in. beyond the end of the blade. Then butt the top end of the saw against the workbench, and flex the frame until the blade fits in the collet. If it's tight enough, it should make a musical note when you pluck it.

A scroll saw would be the next logical step in choosing a tool for marquetry. I use a 20-in. electric scroll saw, which gives me more accuracy and allows me to do bigger designs. For blades, whether you choose a jeweler's saw or a scroll saw, use size 2/0 (2/0, not 2).

An angled table is the key to double-bevel cutting. If I'm cutting $\frac{1}{16}$-in.-thick veneer on a scroll saw, I tilt the table 8°, but the angle might have to be adjusted for

No need to buy veneer. By cutting his own veneer, the author controls the figure of the wood used in the inlays and uses scrap that otherwise might be thrown out. He runs one face of a board over the jointer before cutting the ¹⁄₁₆-in.-thick veneers on a bandsaw.

Cutting technique makes a perfect fit

Background and inlay pieces are stacked together and cut at the same time. Because the edges are beveled, the process ensures a tight fit between adjacent pieces and no visible gluelines in the finished marquetry.

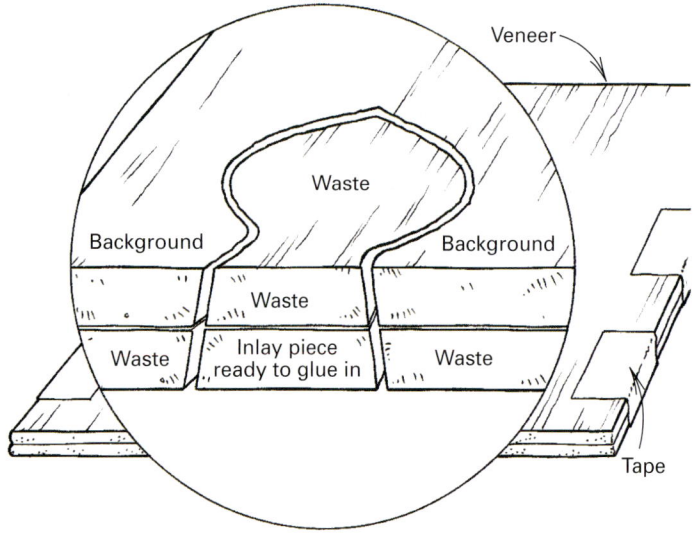

Veneer

Waste

Background | Background

Waste

Waste | Inlay piece ready to glue in | Waste

Tape

veneers of different thickness. If you're using a jeweler's saw, you'll need to make a simple angled table, as shown in the drawing on the facing page. I made mine from ³⁄₄-in. plywood and tilted the top at 8°. I cut a notch, or bird's mouth, in the front edge of the table, as the drawing shows, so the work is supported all around the sawblade. I clamp the table to my bench when I need it and stow it underneath when I don't.

When you're using the jeweler's saw, move the work into the blade, just as you would with a scroll saw. The table holds the work at the correct angle, so keep the saw vertical. You'll probably find it relatively easy to keep the blade from tilting left or right, but you might have to fight the tendency to let the handle of the saw tilt toward you. If your curves consistently come out looking sloppy, this is probably the cause. Make your saw a consistent, smooth, slow-cutting machine that stays in one place at one angle. If your inlay pieces are consistently too tight or too loose, try changing the tilt angle of your table. With the jeweler's saw table, a shim will do the trick. With either the handsaw or scroll saw, keep an eye on any small pieces of veneer. It's easy to lose them.

Start with a simple design

It's time to do some marquetry. First choose a background veneer and a contrasting veneer to inlay into the background. Make a sandwich of the two pieces with the background veneer on top. Tape the veneers together with masking tape. Tape them securely, creasing the tape into the corners with your fingernail. Any movement will distort the final fit of the inlay, so don't reuse the tape.

Draw a design on your background veneer. Except for the simplest designs, I use tracing paper to copy the original. Then I lay the tracing on the veneer with a sheet of carbon or graphite paper between the two and retrace the design, as shown in the top photo on p. 176.

For a start, try something easy like a little blob. I always cut counterclockwise. Because the teeth on the scroll saw face me as I'm cutting, tilting the table down from right to left produces the correct bevel. With the jeweler's saw, the teeth face away from me, so I built the table with the opposite tilt—running downward from left to right.

When you feel more confident, try cutting multicurved blobs and other simple patterns. Now try a point. At the tip of the point, keep your saw moving gently in one spot as you bring the work all the way around. You'll be grinding a small hole, but with practice, the parts will fit correctly.

I need a bunch of clamps, right?

Gluing in the inlay pieces requires no tape and no clamping. Just place the background veneer face down on any flat surface, spread glue on the edges of the inlay piece and press it in from the back (see the bottom right photo on p. 176). The bevel-to-bevel fit provides the only pressure you need. By the time you get the next piece of inlay veneer taped to the background, the glue will have set enough to let you proceed with the sawing.

Overlay and piercing

Marquetry comes alive when one piece is inlaid over another. This is overlay. You can learn the basics of overlay by cutting a bird's head. First draw the outline of a bird's head on your background, and then inlay a beak into the background. Spread glue on the

edges, and press the beak in from the back. Then make the cut for the head through the beak piece, giving a nice crisp edge where the head overlaps, as shown in the top photo on p. 177.

Piercing involves drilling a tiny hole to slip the sawblade through. It's easiest to start all your cuts from an edge of the background, but inevitably, you'll have to drop a piece into the center of a background. Or

A palette of natural woods

Natural wood colors, not stain or dye, offer plenty of variety for eye-catching marquetry.

Darks	Reds	Greens
Ebony	Bloodwood	Olive
Walnut	Pernambuco	Lignum vitae
Wenge	Pear	Greenheart
Imbuia	Bubinga	Tulip poplar

Lights	Yellows	Browns
Pear	Osage orange	Fir
Holly	Satinwood	Lacewood
Maple	Boxwood	Mahogany
Madrone	Lignum vitae	Yew
	Nutmeg	Walnut

Build the cutting table at an angle

When cutting the beveled pieces by hand, results are more accurate when the saw is held straight and the workpieces are at an angle. The author uses a plywood cutting table with a canted top. For veneers 1/16 in. thick, try an 8° angle, and then add shims to the base of the table to adjust the fit of the background and inlay pieces.

5 in.

8° angle

14 in.

Notch

About 6 in.

Shim here if too loose.

Clamp

Shim here if too tight.

Carbon paper for the design. To transfer patterns to the workpiece, the author starts with tracing paper and then uses carbon paper to reproduce the pattern on the veneer he intends to cut.

A drill can help get a cut started. When an inlay must be dropped into the middle of a piece, the author starts the cut with a tiny drill bit.

No tape and no clamps. After pieces have been cut out, the author glues the inlay into the background material from the back side.

you'll want to go back to add a piece after completing a design. That's where piercing comes in.

First I tape the pieces together. Then I use a tiny drill bit in a hand-held pin vise to pierce both veneers. Drill at one tip of the piece to be cut out (see the bottom left photo below). Release the blade from the top of your saw, and gently slip the blade through the hole in the underside of the bottom veneer. Reattach the blade, and cut out the design. This leaves a small hole in one corner of the pattern. It can be well-hidden with a mix of sawdust and glue.

Shading with hot sand

This last trick—sand shading—really adds depth and shadow to your design, as the flower in the bottom photo at right on the facing page shows. Wash some fairly fine sand, and heat it up on a hot plate. Pick up the inlay piece that needs a little shading with a pair of tweezers. Then dip an edge of the piece into the sand, as shown in the bottom left photo on the facing page.

Check the inlay piece constantly because once the wood starts to toast, it darkens quickly. Be careful not to toast large pieces of veneer for too long because they have a tendency to shrink in the heat and distort the fit.

Finishing up

When your marquetry is finished, glue it down to a plywood core at least $1/8$ in. thick. And always glue veneer to the back of the core simultaneously to keep the stresses balanced and the core flat. I put a layer of cardboard on the marquetry and stack a few inches of particleboard on top when I clamp the veneer. Then I use as many clamps as I can fit.

After sanding, I finish with shellac because it doesn't distort the color of the wood too much. It's magic when you put on the first coat and the contrasts jump out at you. In this medium, you get textures, pores, colors and light reflections. That is really what makes marquetry so special.

First the beak, then the head. Crisp boundaries are achieved by overlaying one part of a pattern into another, as the author is doing with this bird's beak and head. The scroll-saw table is tilted at 8°.

Petals are cut in one at a time. Crisp boundaries between individual petals in this sample piece enhance the image's three-dimensional feel.

Hot sand for subtle shading. The finished flower at right gets a sense of visual depth from the shading between adjacent petals. To achieve the effect, the author uses hot sand to scorch the edges of some of the pieces. But be careful—too much heat on large pieces of veneer will change the fit.

ABOUT THE AUTHORS

Christian Becksvoort is a long-time cabinetmaker in the Shaker style and a contributing editor to *Fine Woodworking* magazine. He is the author of *The Shaker Legacy*.

Mike Burton recently handed over the operation of his furniture company to his sons. Now semi-retired, he still takes on some carving and turning commissions but spends most of his time working as a photographer and freelance writer for woodworking publications. For the most part self-taught: He says he's a student of the School of Hard Knocks, but has not yet received his degree. He lives in Ogden, Utah.

Jack Danilchak's woodshop is in Smithton, Penn. Along with various pieces of furniture, he builds presentation boxes for miniature, fully working rifles, machined by a gunsmith in his area.

Sam Fletcher, of Mechanicsville, Va., started buying power tools and making furniture in 1943, and he's still at it.

Garrett Hack opened his own shop in 1973 and later studied furnituremaking at Boston University's Program in Artisanry. He designs and builds furniture in Vermont and is a regular contributor to *Fine Woodworking* magazine. He is the author of *The Handplane Book* and *Classic Hand Tools*.

Robert Judd is a professional furniture repairer and refinisher in Canton, Mass.

Tony Konovaloff has been making furniture by hand since 1986. He wrote a book, *Chisel, Mallet, Plane and Saw*, about the way he works and how he makes his furniture. He lives with his wife and three sons in Oak Harbor, Wash.

Before **Steven Lamont** turned to woodworking, he served as an Air Force pilot during the Vietnam conflict, and then worked as a private jet pilot for a major corporation. In 1986, he trained for a year with Christopher Faulkner in Devon, England, then returned to Lewisburg, Penn., to make furniture. Now he's employed as a craftsman-tutor at the Edward Barnsley Educational Trust, and lives with his wife and three children in Hampshire, England.

Steve Latta has spent most of his career specializing in inlay and marquetry. Recently he shifted gears and became an instructor at the Thaddeus Steven College of Technology in Lancaster, Penn. The job leaves him time to take on only an occasional woodworking commission. When he goes home and plays dad to a newborn, a toddler, and a first-grader, his focus shifts from Sheraton to Suess.

John Lively is editor-in-chief and vice president of The Taunton Press.

Phil Lowe has operated a furnituremaking and restoration shop in Beverly, Mass., since 1985. Before that, he was an instructor and department head at the North Bennett Street School for 10 years. He has been woodworking since 1968. Phil has written many articles for *Fine Woodworking,* made several videos, and been a guest speaker and demonstrator at various trade shows, and schools. He continues his commitment to teaching by taking students year-round.

Nigel Martin is a professional cabinetmaker in Norfolk, England.

Patrick Nelson designs and builds furniture professionally in Fulton, Mo. David Mount, an amateur woodworker in Two Harbors, Minn., assisted in the writing of the article that begins on p. 12.

Alan Peters first began woodworking as an apprentice in Edward Barnsley's workshop in 1949. He has been designing and building furniture ever since. In 1990, he received the OBE (Order of the British Empire) from the queen of England for his contributions as a designer and craftsman. He lives and works in Kentisbeare, Devon, England, where he manages a team of four other craftsmen.

Bruce Peterson works in a one-man shop in Pilar, N.M.

Frank Pollaro teaches workshops on veneering and is a designer and builder of fine furniture in East Orange, N.J.

Mario Rodriguez is a contributing editor to *Fine Woodworking* magazine and woodworker living in Haddonfield, N.J. He teaches toolmaking, furnituremaking, and antique restoration at the Fashion Institute of Design in New York City. He is the author of *Traditional Woodwork.*

Gary Rogowski has been building furniture in Portland, Oreg., since 1974. His design work has been shown in galleries nation-

wide. A contributing editor to *Fine Woodworking* magazine and the author of *Router Joinery,* he has taught classes and workshop around the country. He now operates his own school, the Northwest Woodworking Studio, which promotes an appreciation of the craft through hands-on education.

Gary Straub is a professional woodworker living in furniture in Columbia, Mo.

Lindsay Suter is an architect and furniture-maker in New Haven, Conn., where he emphasizes ecological sustainability in his practice. His latest project, combining architecture and woodworking, is a monument to the millennium in Dorchester, England, for Prince Charles.

Malcolm Vaughan left a career in journalism and public relations in 1984 to pursue a more tangible, creative, and satisfying career as a woodworker. He apprenticed with David Charlesworth and David Savage, then set up his own business in 1988. His counts Shaker and Arts and Crafts among the influences on his designs. He lives in Biddeford, Devon, England.

Gregg Zall operates a one-man shop in Petaluma, Calif., specializing in marquetry and inlay furniture. He currently teaches at the California College of Arts and Crafts, College of the Redwoods Fine Woodworking Program, and the Randall Museum.

CREDITS

Vince Babak (illustrator): pp. 68, 94, 95, 97, 99, 107-109

Jonathan Binzen (photographer): pp. 76-78, 172-176

Jim Boesel (photographer): pp. 50, 51

Anatole Burkin (photographer): pp. 38-43

William Duckworth (photographer): pp. 74, 86-88, 90-92, 100, 107, 109, 112-117

Aimé Fraser (photographer): pp. 93, 96-98

Tony Freeman-Cosh (photographer): p. 18

Michael Gellatly (illustrator): pp. 25-27, 29, 154, 155

Scott Gibson (photographer): pp. 138, 141-145

Dennis Griggs (photographer): pp. 13, 124-127

Boyd Haden (photographer): pp. 79-85

Lee Hov (illustrator): pp. 19, 20

Sloan Howard (photographer): p. 151

Susan Kahn (photographer): pp. 128, 129, 152

John Kelley (photographer): pp. 56-61

Peter Krumhardt (photographer): pp. 12, 15-17

Blair Kunz (photographer): p. 140

Heather Lambert (illustrator): pp. 53, 77, 162, 163

Bob LaPoint (illustrator): pp. 13, 14, 111

Vincent Laurence (photographer): pp. 4, 6, 7, 9, 11, 31, 36, 44, 48, 49, 54, 63-69, 102-106, 156, 157, 162-164, 166, 167

Nigel Martin (photographer): pp. 21, 23

Dennis Preston (photographer): pp. 118, 133-137

Michael Pekovich (illustrator): pp. 125

Scott Phillips (photographer): pp. 134, 160, 161

Jim Richey (illustrator): pp. 8, 10, 32, 34, 40

Charley Robinson (photographer): p. 2, 24, 26-28, 70-73, 120-122, 132

Kathleeen Rushton (illustrator): p. 131

Mark Sant'Angelo (illustrator): p. 57

Gary Straub (photographer): pp. 158, 168-171

Mike Wanke (illustrator): pp. 174, 175

Alec Waters (photographer): pp. 30, 31, 33-35, 146-148, 150

Matthew Wells (illustrator): pp. 45-47

EQUIVALENCE CHART

Inches	Centimeters	Millimeters	Inches	Centimeters	Millimeters
$1/8$	0.3	3	12	30.5	305
$1/4$	0.6	6	13	33.0	330
$3/8$	1.0	10	14	35.6	356
$1/2$	1.3	13	15	38.1	381
$5/8$	1.6	16	16	40.6	406
$3/4$	1.9	19	17	43.2	432
$7/8$	2.2	22	18	45.7	457
1	2.5	25	19	48.3	483
$1 1/4$	3.2	32	20	50.8	508
$1 1/2$	3.8	38	21	53.3	533
$1 3/4$	4.4	44	22	55.9	559
2	5.1	51	23	58.4	584
$2 1/2$	6.4	64	24	61.0	610
3	7.6	76	25	63.5	635
$3 1/2$	8.9	89	26	66.0	660
4	10.2	102	27	68.6	686
$4 1/2$	11.4	114	28	71.1	711
5	12.7	127	29	73.7	737
6	15.2	152	30	76.2	762
7	17.8	178	31	78.7	787
8	20.3	203	32	81.3	813
9	22.9	229	33	83.8	838
10	25.4	254	34	86.4	864
11	27.9	279	35	88.9	889
			36	91.4	914

INDEX

Publisher: Jim Childs

Associate Publisher: Helen Albert

Associate Editor: Strother Purdy

Designer: Amy Bernard Russo

Layout Artist: Susan Fazekas

Indexer: Harriet Hodges

Fine Woodworking magazine

Editor: Timothy D. Schreiner

Art Director: Bob Goodfellow

Managing Editor: Jefferson Kolle

Senior Editors: Jonathan Binzen, Anatole Burkin

Associate Editor: William Duckworth

Assistant Editor: Matthew Teague

Associate Art Director: Michael Pekovich